POSITIVE PARENTING CONNECTION AND SETTING LIMITS

TEACH CHILDREN RESPONSIBILITY, PROBLEM-SOLVING, AND COOPERATION

DDJ PUBLISHING

CONTENTS

Introduction   5

1. SETTING LIMITS   11
   Strategies for Setting Limits   12
   When to Be Flexible   14
   Avoiding Nagging   16
   How to Set Limits for Development   18
   Enforcing the New Limits   20
   Adjusting to the Changes   24

2. CONNECTION VERSUS
   CONTROLLING   31
   Managing Emotions and Difficult
   Situations   37
   Building a Safe and Supportive
   Environment   44

3. FIGHT OR FLIGHT   51
   What Is the Limbic System?   52
   Mirror Neurons   59
   Calming the Situation   60
   The Calm After the Storm   62

4. STAY WITH THEM CLOSELY   69
   The Importance of Crying   72
   Learning to Self-Regulate   77
   Eye Contact   82

5. DO NOT LECTURE   87
   Appreciate Our Differences   89
   Less Is More   91

How to Stop Lecturing   93
The Importance of Communication and
the Words We Use   100

6. ENCOURAGEMENT INSTEAD OF
PRAISE   105
What Is the Difference Between Praise
and Encouragement?   106
How We Choose Words   108
Finding the Balance   110
Acknowledging a Child's Efforts   114

7. CONSEQUENCES WITH EMPATHY   125
What Are the Consequences of Empathy?   126
How to Support Our Children Through
Consequences With Empathy?   128
Imposing Consequences   131
The Impact of Criticism   136
Embracing Mistakes and Failure   140

8. ROLE MODELING   145
How to Be an Effective Role Model   147
Modeling for Our Children in Practical
Life   149
The Importance of Explanations   153

9. LEARNING TO CHOOSE CREATES
RESPONSIBILITY   157
How to Teach Responsibility Through
Choices   161
Testing the Boundaries   164

Conclusion   169
References   173

INTRODUCTION

After working a busy long weekend up in New York, I was excited to be spending some time with our family and friends for the rest of the week. Our friends are lucky enough to be blessed with a gorgeous 15-month-old son who continues to baffle us all every single day with his independence and a zest for life I think you can only really see in toddlers these days.

During my stay with our friends, I was blessed to see our three children interact together and I could instantly see the fruits of our labors over the months and years of parenting these wonderful children. Any tantrums were quickly diffused by a short reminder of the expectations and limits we had for them. During the entire week, I do not recall one instance where any of the adults needed to react in a harsh or loud way. We are lucky enough to share very similar parenting beliefs and styles with our friends, which also meant we were spending the week in a space that was already ideal for our children to be themselves.

On our return home, we were preparing to board the plane when I heard a family nearby erupting into a screaming match because of a disagreement between their two children. The parents were obviously flustered and embarrassed, while their children were overstimulated and exhausted. As I sat down with my family, I felt a sudden wave of calm wash over us all. You could tell that all four of us felt grateful to have already discussed our expectations, limits, and boundaries for the whole trip. My partner and I have already had many long conversations on how we handle difficult situations with our children in public and at home, which allows us to feel confident in how we handle pretty much anything parenthood throws at us. Our kids are reassured that they already know what is happening and what will happen. They enjoy the security of consistent consequences and know that we are there for them whenever they need us, but they also have the independence to sort many things out for themselves. They have already learned so many skills just from how we have chosen to run our home and for that, my family is so grateful. It is because of this confidence and my family feeling so thankful that I am excited to share this knowledge with you. I want every family to have a healthy relationship so we can all navigate this crazy world with the security of a strong family unit.

Welcome to the world of positive parenting! As a parent, you have the important and rewarding job of guiding and nurturing your child's development. One of the key aspects of positive parenting is setting limits, which can help your child feel safe, secure, and understood, and can also provide them with a clear model for acceptable behavior.

But setting limits can be challenging, especially if you're not sure where to start. In this book, we'll explore the importance of setting limits in parenting, and we'll offer practical tips and strategies for setting and enforcing limits in a positive and effective way.

So, why are limits important in parenting? First and foremost, limits help children feel safe and secure. Children crave structure and predictability, and setting clear boundaries and expectations can provide them with a sense of stability and security. When children know what is expected of them, they are more likely to feel confident and secure in their environment.

In addition to promoting emotional security, setting limits can also encourage self-control and independence. When children understand that there are consequences for not following rules, they are more likely to think before they act and consider the consequences of their actions. This can help them learn to regulate their own behavior and make responsible decisions.

Setting limits can also increase self-esteem, as children learn to follow rules and meet expectations. And when children are faced with limits, they may need to come up with creative ways to solve problems or find alternative ways to achieve their goals, which can help them develop problem-solving skills and critical thinking abilities.

Finally, setting and enforcing limits can help improve relationships between parents and children. When children understand the expectations and consequences of their behavior, they are more likely to respect their parents and have a more positive relationship with them.

So, now that we've discussed the importance of setting limits in parenting, let's talk about how to do it effectively. One key aspect of positive parenting is using positive language and reinforcing positive behavior. This means focusing on what you want your child to do, rather than what you don't want them to do. For example, instead of saying "Don't run," try saying "Please walk." Using positive language can be more effective at redirecting behavior and can help your child feel valued and supported.

Another important aspect of positive parenting is setting clear and consistent expectations. Make sure that your child understands the rules and expectations you have set for them, and be consistent in your communication and enforcement of those rules. This can help your child feel more secure and can encourage positive behavior.

It's also important to be patient and understanding when setting and enforcing limits. Children may need time to adjust to new rules, and it's natural for them to test limits as they learn and grow. Be patient and offer support and guidance.

Let's dive in and start tackling some of the trickiest parenting situations with positive parenting solutions you can use to navigate almost any situation. Together, we will all be able to make parenting a little less stressful so we can all enjoy watching our children grow into young adults. We will start our journey with the importance of setting limits, enforcing our limits, and how to grow and change our limits with our growing families.

1

SETTING LIMITS

Becoming a parent is a common experience for most adults, but it can also be challenging and frustrating. The various stages of children's development present different difficulties, but the good news is that there are research-based strategies and tools now available to help parents navigate these challenges, such as child tantrums, behavior problems, bedtime issues, selective eating, and risk-taking. Positive psychology, with its focus on happiness, positive youth development, resilience, and well-being, is especially relevant in the context of positive parenting. Whether you're looking to prevent potential challenges or are already dealing with a difficult situation, understanding and utilizing the principles of positive psychology can help you become a more effective and successful parent.

The benefits of setting limits with young children include promoting emotional security and self-control, independence, and also helping them to understand the consequences of their actions. Setting clear boundaries and expectations can provide children with a sense of stability and security. Parents should communicate their expectations clearly and consistently, and enforce consequences consistently when necessary to avoid nagging. It is also important to remember that setting limits can be challenging and it may require a balance of flexibility and consistency.

However, positive parenting is not all about positivity. You will have to start setting and enforcing limits for your child to build and maintain an appropriate and functional parent-child relationship. Let's look into how we can start setting those limits to make parenting a whole lot more positive!

STRATEGIES FOR SETTING LIMITS

There are a few strategies that parents can use to effectively set limits with young children:

- **Communicate expectations clearly and consistently**: Make sure that your children understand the rules and expectations you have

POSITIVE PARENTING CONNECTION AND SETTING LI... | 13

set for them. Use age-appropriate language and be clear and consistent in your communication.

- **Use positive reinforcement**: When children follow the rules and meet expectations, make sure to praise and reward their behavior. This can help reinforce the desired behavior and encourage children to continue following the rules.

- **Set appropriate consequences**: When children do not follow the rules, it is important to set appropriate consequences that are consistent with the behavior. Make sure that the consequences are related to the behavior and that they are not too harsh or severe.

- **Use natural consequences**: When appropriate, allow children to experience the natural consequences of their actions. For example, if a child refuses to put on a coat when it is cold outside, allow them to feel the natural consequence of being cold. This can help children understand the cause and effect of their actions and encourage them to make better decisions in the future.

- **Limit distractions**: Minimize distractions that may make it more difficult for children to follow the rules. For example, if you are trying to have a conversation with your child, turn off the television or move to a quieter location to reduce distractions.

In conclusion, setting limits is an important aspect of parenting young children. It helps children feel emotionally secure, promotes self-control and independence, and encourages responsible decision-making. By communicating expectations clearly and consistently, using positive reinforcement, setting appropriate consequences, and limiting distractions, parents can effectively set and enforce limits with their young children.

It is important for parents to be flexible and adjust rules when necessary, as this can help children feel understood and supported, and it can also help parents respond effectively to changing circumstances and situations. However, it is important for parents to be mindful of when it is appropriate to be flexible and adjust rules, as maintaining consistency and structure is also important for children's development.

WHEN TO BE FLEXIBLE

Here are a few considerations for when it might be appropriate for parents to be flexible and adjust rules:

- **When the rule is no longer relevant**: As children grow and develop, their needs and abilities change. It may be appropriate to adjust rules as children grow and mature, or as circumstances change. For example, a rule that was appropriate for a toddler may no longer be relevant for a school-aged child.

- **When the rule is causing undue stress or conflict**: If a rule is causing undue stress or conflict within the family, it may be appropriate to revisit the rule and consider adjusting it. It is important for parents to be mindful of the impact that their rules and expectations have on their children and to make adjustments as needed to promote a healthy and positive family dynamic.

- **If the rule is not being followed consistently**: If a rule is not being followed consistently or is being enforced unfairly, it may be appropriate to revisit the rule and consider adjusting it. It is important for parents to be consistent in their communication and enforcement of rules in order to be effective.

- **If the rule is not in line with the child's developmental stage**: Children's developmental stages can have a significant impact on their ability to understand and follow rules. It may be appropriate for parents to adjust rules or expectations in response to a child's developmental needs and abilities.

In summary, it is important for parents to be flexible and adjust rules when necessary, but it is also important to maintain consistency and structure in order to support children's development. Parents should consider the specific needs and abilities of their children and the impact that rules and expectations have on the family dynamic when determining when to be flexible and adjust rules.

Constant complaints and negative interactions can cause frustration for both parents and children and can weaken the ability to establish and uphold rules and boundaries. It is important for parents to be clear and direct with their children about how they want them to behave, and to communicate expectations in a calm and positive way.

AVOIDING NAGGING

Here are a few strategies for avoiding nagging and negative interactions when setting and maintaining expectations and limits:

- **Be clear and specific:** Make sure that your children understand the rules and expectations you have set for them. Use age-appropriate language and be clear and specific about what you expect.

- **Use positive reinforcement:** When children follow the rules and meet expectations, make sure to praise and reward their behavior. This can help reinforce the desired behavior and encourage children to continue following the rules.

- **Set appropriate consequences:** When children do not follow the rules, it is important to set appropriate consequences that are consistent with the behavior. Make sure that the consequences are related to the behavior and that they are not too harsh or severe.

- **Avoid lecturing or nagging:** Nagging or lecturing can be frustrating for children and can undermine the effectiveness of the limits being set. Instead, calmly and clearly communicate the expectations and consequences, and allow children to learn from the natural consequences of their actions.

- **Stay calm:** It is important for parents to stay calm and composed when communicating expectations and setting limits. Children are more likely to respond positively and follow rules when they feel that their parents are calm and in control.

By being clear and direct, using positive reinforcement, setting appropriate consequences, avoiding nagging or lecturing, and staying calm, parents can effectively set and maintain expectations and limits with their children without resorting to negative interactions. This can help create a positive and respectful family dynamic and improve relationships between parents and children.

A child's ability to accept limits is an essential part of their learning and development process. When children understand and accept the limits that are set for them, they are better able to make good choices and understand the consequences of their actions.

HOW TO SET LIMITS FOR DEVELOPMENT

Here are a few ways that the limit-setting process can help children develop their ability to make good choices:

- **Promotes self-control and independence**: When children understand and accept the limits that are set for them, they are more likely to develop self-control and independence. They learn to regulate their own behavior and make responsible decisions, rather than relying on others to control their actions.

- **Encourages responsible decision-making**: As children learn to understand and accept limits, they are also more likely to consider the consequences of their actions before making a decision. This can help them make more responsible and thoughtful choices.

- **Increases understanding of cause and effect**: When children experience the consequences of their actions, they are more likely to understand the cause and effect of their behavior. This can help them make better decisions in the future.

- **Develop problem-solving skills**: When children are faced with limits, they may need to come up with creative ways to solve problems or find alternative ways to achieve their goals. This can help them develop problem-solving skills and critical thinking abilities.

In conclusion, the limit-setting process is an important part of a child's learning and development. By setting clear limits and expectations and consistently enforcing consequences, parents can help their children develop self-control, independence, and responsible decision-making skills.

Children feel more emotionally secure when they know what they can and cannot do, and when they understand that their parents are in control and can enforce limits consistently. Setting clear and meaningful boundaries for children's behavior helps them understand what is expected of them and provides them with a sense of structure and predictability.

When parents are unable to set and enforce limits consistently, children may lose respect for their parents and may develop patterns of misbehaving without facing consequences. This can lead to increased insecurity and can have negative impacts on children's relationships with their parents and others.

ENFORCING THE NEW LIMITS

Here are a few strategies for setting and enforcing limits with children:

- **Communicate expectations clearly and consistently**: Make sure that your children understand the rules and expectations you have set for them. Use age-appropriate language and be clear and consistent in your communication.

- **Use positive reinforcement**: When children follow the rules and meet expectations, make sure to praise and reward their behavior. This can help reinforce the desired behavior and encourage children to continue following the rules.

- **Set appropriate consequences**: When children do not follow the rules, it is important to set appropriate consequences that are consistent with the behavior. Make sure that the consequences are related to the behavior and that they are not too harsh or severe.

- **Enforce consequences consistently**: It is important to enforce consequences consistently when children do not follow the rules. This helps children understand that their actions have consequences and helps them learn to make responsible decisions.

By setting clear and meaningful boundaries and consistently enforcing consequences, parents can help their children feel emotionally secure and develop patterns of responsible behavior. This can lead to increased self-control, independence, and healthy relationships.

It is always better to model to your child how to use household items and toys for their intended purposes. There are a few strategies that parents can use to show children how to use household items and toys for their intended purpose:

- **Demonstrate proper use**: Show children how to use household items and toys correctly by demonstrating the proper use. For example, if you are teaching a child how to use a hammer, show them how to hold the hammer, how to line up the nail, and how to strike the nail with the hammer.
- **Use age-appropriate language**: When explaining how to use household items and toys, use age-appropriate language that the child can understand. Avoid using technical terms or jargon that may be confusing.
- **Use visual aids**: Visual aids, such as pictures or videos, can be helpful for demonstrating the proper use of household items and toys.
- **Provide supervision**: It is important to provide supervision when children are using household items and toys, especially if they are using them for the first time. This can help ensure that they are using the items safely and correctly.
- **Encourage practice**: Encourage children to practice using household items and toys in a safe and controlled environment. This can help them develop their skills and confidence.

By demonstrating proper use, using age-appropriate language, using visual aids, providing supervision, and encouraging practice, parents can effectively show children how to use household items and toys for their intended purpose.

Using positive language is an effective way to redirect a child's behavior and encourage positive behavior. Positive language focuses on the desired behavior, rather than the negative behavior, and it helps children feel valued and supported.

Here are a few strategies for using positive language to redirect a child's behavior:

- **Use "I" statements**: Instead of saying "You're not listening," try saying "I need you to listen to me." "I" statements help to avoid accusations and can be more effective at redirecting behavior.
- **Use positive phrases**: Instead of saying "Don't run," try saying "Please walk." Positive phrases focus on the desired behavior and can be more effective at redirecting behavior.
- **Use praise**: When children display positive behavior, make sure to praise and reward their behavior. This can encourage them to continue displaying positive behavior.

- **Avoid negative phrases**: Avoid using negative phrases such as "don't" or "stop," as they can be confusing and may not be effective at redirecting behavior.

By using "I" statements, positive phrases, praise, and avoiding negative phrases, parents can effectively redirect a child's behavior using positive language. This can help children feel valued and supported, and it can encourage positive behavior.

When setting new limits or boundaries, it is important to allow yourself and your child plenty of time to adjust to the changes. This can help ensure a smooth transition and can minimize frustration and stress.

ADJUSTING TO THE CHANGES

Here are a few strategies for allowing yourself and your child plenty of time to make adjustments when setting new limits or boundaries:

- **Communicate clearly**: Make sure to clearly communicate the new limits or boundaries to your child and explain the reasons behind them. This can help your child understand the changes and feel more comfortable with them.

- **Be patient**: It may take time for your child to adjust to the new limits or boundaries, so it is important to be patient and understanding during the transition. Encourage your child to express any concerns or frustrations they may have, and offer support and guidance as needed.
- **Gradually introduce changes**: Instead of making all of the changes at once, consider introducing them gradually. This can give you and your child time to adjust to the changes and can make the transition easier.
- **Offer support and encouragement**: Offer your child support and encouragement as they adjust to the new limits or boundaries. Let them know that you are there to help them navigate the changes and that you believe in their ability to adapt.

By communicating clearly, being patient, gradually introducing changes, and offering support and encouragement, parents can help themselves and their children adjust to new limits or boundaries. This can help ensure a smooth transition and can minimize frustration and stress.

Choosing limits for a child can be challenging, as it is important to consider the child's age, maturity, and individual needs and abilities. Here are a few factors to consider when choosing limits for a child:

- **Developmental stage**: Children's developmental stages can have a significant impact on their ability to understand and follow rules. It is important to consider a child's developmental stage when choosing limits, as younger children may need more guidance and structure than older children.
- **Individual needs and abilities**: Every child is different, and it is important to consider a child's individual needs and abilities when choosing limits. For example, a child with special needs may require different limits than a child without special needs.
- **Family values and goals**: It is important to consider the values and goals of the family when choosing limits for a child. For example, if the family values education, it may be appropriate to set limits around screen time in order to prioritize homework and schoolwork.
- **Safety**: Safety should always be a top priority when choosing limits for a child. Make sure to set limits that protect children from harm and ensure their safety.

- **Age-appropriateness**: It is important to choose limits that are age-appropriate for children. For example, a limit that is appropriate for a toddler may not be appropriate for a school-aged child.

By considering the child's developmental stage, individual needs and abilities, family values and goals, safety, and age-appropriateness, parents can effectively choose limits that are appropriate for their child.

It is important to clearly and effectively communicate the limits that are set for children in order to help them understand and follow the rules. Here are a few strategies for informing children about the limits set for them:

- **Explain the reasons behind the limits**: Help children understand the reasons behind the limits by explaining the purpose and rationale for the rules. This can help children feel understood and can encourage their cooperation.
- **Set clear and consistent expectations**: Make sure that the limits you set are clear and consistent, and that children understand what is expected of them.
- **Use positive language**: Use positive language to communicate the limits, rather than focusing

on negative behavior. For example, instead of saying, "Don't run," try saying, "Please walk."

- **Provide examples**: Provide examples of the desired behavior to help children understand what is expected of them. For example, if you are setting a limit around screen time, you might say, "We have a rule that screen time is limited to two hours per day. That means you can watch one hour of TV in the morning and one hour in the evening."

In this chapter on setting limits, parents learn about the importance of establishing boundaries for their children in order to teach them responsibility and self-discipline. Setting limits helps children learn to make appropriate choices and understand the consequences of their actions. This chapter may also discuss techniques for setting and enforcing limits, such as natural consequences, logical consequences, and redirecting behavior.

In the next chapter on connection versus controlling, parents explore the difference between being controlling and being connected with their children. Parents learn that when they are too controlling, they risk undermining their child's sense of autonomy and self-esteem. On the other hand, when they are connected, they create a sense of trust and understanding with their child, which leads to greater cooperation and open communication. The next chapter may also delve into how to be a supportive and available parent while still allowing children to make mistakes and learn from them, and how to navigate discipline with balance, both connection, and control where needed.

2

CONNECTION VERSUS CONTROLLING

When it comes to parenting, the terms "connection" and "control" often come up in discussions about how to best support and guide children. Connection refers to the emotional bond that parents and children share, while control refers to the actions and strategies parents use to shape their children's behavior.

In many ways, these two concepts are closely related. A strong emotional connection between parents and children can help facilitate cooperation and positive behavior, while a lack of connection can make it more difficult for parents to effectively control their children's behavior.

On the other hand, too much emphasis on control can undermine the emotional connection between parents and children. Children who feel controlled may feel resentful or unsupported, which can lead to defiance and other negative behaviors.

Finding the right balance between connection and control is an ongoing process, and it can be challenging for parents. In this chapter, we will explore different strategies for building a strong emotional connection with your children while also setting clear boundaries and expectations for behavior. We will also examine common challenges that parents face when trying to strike this balance and explore ways to navigate these challenges effectively.

Ultimately, the goal of parenting is to raise children who are happy, healthy, and well-adjusted. By fostering a strong emotional connection with your children and setting appropriate boundaries, you can help them develop the skills and resilience they need to thrive in the world.

It is normal for parents to want to be in control and to manage situations involving their children. It is important for parents to provide guidance and support to their children as they grow and develop. However, it is also important for parents to allow their children to have some independence and to make their own mistakes, as this is a crucial part of the learning and growing process. It is important for parents to strike a balance between providing support and guidance, and allowing their children the freedom to make their own decisions and learn from their mistakes.

It is natural for parents to want to help their children when they are struggling to manage their emotions. However, it is important for parents to allow their children to learn how to regulate their emotions on their own. By stepping in and "doing it for them," parents may inadvertently prevent their children from developing their own emotional regulation skills. Over time, this can lead to an inability to manage emotions independently, as well as resentment from the child. Instead of "controlling" the situation, it can be more helpful for parents to provide support and guidance to their children as they learn to regulate their emotions. This can involve teaching coping strategies, such as deep breathing or counting to ten, and modeling healthy emotional expression. It can also involve helping children to identify and name their emotions, and to understand that it is okay to feel a range of emotions.

It is important for parents to provide emotional support to their children, particularly when they are experiencing distress. When children feel connected to their parents and know that they are there to support them, they are more likely to feel secure and confident. This can help them to think for themselves and to tap into their own mental and emotional resources. Providing emotional support involves being present and available to listen and offer guidance and understanding. It also involves showing empathy and validation, and helping children to feel seen and heard. When children feel supported emotionally, they are better able to manage their emotions and cope with challenges.

Providing emotional support to children can involve several different things, including:

- **Being present and available to listen**: This involves giving children your full attention when they need to talk, and showing that you are interested in what they have to say.
- **Offering guidance and understanding**: This involves helping children to understand their emotions and to find healthy ways to cope with them.
- **Showing empathy and validation**: This involves acknowledging and understanding the feelings that children are experiencing and letting them know that their feelings are valid and important.

- **Helping children to feel seen and heard**: This involves letting children know that their thoughts and feelings matter, and that you are there to listen and support them.

It is important for parents to provide emotional support to their children on an ongoing basis, not just in times of distress. When children feel emotionally supported, they are more likely to feel confident and capable and to develop healthy coping skills. By providing emotional support to children and helping them to develop healthy coping skills, parents can encourage their children to become more self-sufficient and confident.

It is important for parents to work collaboratively with their children to help them manage their emotions. Instead of simply controlling or correcting their behavior, it can be more effective to involve children in finding solutions to problems and helping them to develop their own coping strategies. By listening to children and involving them in the process of finding solutions, parents can help children to feel heard and valued, which can in turn help them to feel more in control of their emotions. Collaborative problem-solving can also help children to develop their decision-making skills and to become more self-sufficient. When parents offer a collaborative approach, children are more likely to listen and be receptive to guidance and feedback.

Developing cooperative skills can be an important part of helping children to manage their emotions and to address issues in a healthy way. When children have the skills to communicate effectively and to work collaboratively with others, they are better able to regulate their emotions and resolve conflicts. These skills can also help children to feel more confident and to have higher self-esteem, as they feel more capable of managing their own emotions and navigating social situations. Cooperative skills can be taught and reinforced through modeling, practice, and positive reinforcement. As children develop these skills, they will have the resources they need to avoid more negative or aggressive behaviors, and to handle difficult situations in a more positive way.

It is important for parents to create a strong connection with their children in order to effectively influence their behavior. When children feel a sense of connection and safety with their parents, they are more likely to be open to guidance and feedback. On the other hand, punishment, lecturing, nagging, scolding, blaming, or shaming can create negative emotions and may lead to behaviors such as fighting, fleeing, or freezing. Instead of focusing on punishment or correction, it can be more effective to first focus on creating a positive connection with children and building trust. This can involve expressing love and affection, and showing understanding and empathy. Using positive discipline techniques, such as being kind and firm at the same time, can also be helpful in setting boundaries and expectations while maintaining a positive connection with children.

MANAGING EMOTIONS AND DIFFICULT SITUATIONS

Providing children with tools and strategies to manage their emotions and navigate difficult situations can be an important part of strengthening the parent-child connection. When children feel that their parents believe in them and trust them, they are more likely to feel confident and capable. This can lead to greater self-sufficiency and improved relationships with parents and others. Some ways that parents can help their children to develop these skills include:

- **Teaching coping strategies**: This can involve helping children to develop techniques such as deep breathing, counting to ten, or using positive self-talk to manage their emotions.

- **Encouraging open communication**: This can involve creating an open and accepting environment where children feel comfortable talking about their thoughts and feelings.
- **Validating and acknowledging emotions**: This can involve acknowledging and understanding the emotions that children are experiencing and letting them know that their feelings are valid and normal.
- **Providing support and guidance**: This can involve being present and available to listen and offer help when needed, and helping children to navigate challenges and make healthy decisions.

By providing children with the tools and support they need to manage their emotions and navigate difficult situations, parents can help their children to grow and develop self-sufficiency, and build stronger relationships with others.

There are many ways that parents can help their children to develop the skills they need to manage their emotions and navigate difficult situations. Some additional strategies include:

- **Modeling healthy emotional expression**: Children learn by example, so it is important for parents to model healthy emotional expression. This can involve showing children how to identify and express their emotions in a healthy way. It is important for parents to model healthy emotional expressions for their children. This can involve showing children how to identify and name their emotions and express them in a healthy way. It is important for parents to show children that it is okay to feel a range of emotions and to teach them how to manage their emotions in appropriate ways. This can involve demonstrating healthy ways of expressing emotions, such as talking about feelings or using art or play to express emotions. It can also involve modeling healthy coping strategies, such as deep breathing or taking a break to calm down when feeling overwhelmed. By modeling healthy emotional expression, parents can help their children to develop their own emotional intelligence and to understand and manage their emotions in healthy ways.

- **Encouraging self-reflection**: Helping children to think about their feelings and behaviors can be an important part of developing emotional intelligence. Parents can encourage self-reflection by asking open-ended questions and helping children to think about the causes and consequences of their actions. Encouraging self-reflection can be an important part of helping children to develop emotional intelligence and to understand and manage their emotions. Self-reflection involves thinking about one's own feelings and behaviors and considering the causes and consequences of those actions. Parents can encourage self-reflection by asking open-ended questions and helping children to think about their emotions and behaviors. This can involve asking questions such as, "How did you feel when that happened?"; "What do you think caused that reaction?"; or "What could you do differently next time?" Asking open-ended questions can help children to think more deeply about their emotions and behaviors, and to develop their own insights and understanding. By encouraging self-reflection, parents can help children to become more self-aware and to develop the skills they need to manage their emotions in healthy ways.

- **Teaching problem-solving skills**: Helping children to develop problem-solving skills can be an important part of helping them to manage their emotions and navigate difficult situations. Parents can teach these skills through practice and by providing guidance and support. Teaching problem-solving skills can be an important part of helping children to develop emotional intelligence and to manage their emotions in healthy ways. Problem-solving skills involve the ability to identify and solve problems in a logical and strategic way. Parents can help children to develop these skills by providing guidance and support and by encouraging them to practice problem-solving on their own. Some ways that parents can do this include:

○ Modeling problem-solving: Parents can demonstrate how to identify and solve problems by working through problems together and discussing the steps involved. Encouraging independent problem-solving: Parents can encourage children to try to solve problems on their own and to think through the steps involved.

○ Providing support and guidance: When children are stuck or need help, parents can offer support and guidance to help them find solutions.

○ Encouraging creative thinking: Parents can encourage children to think outside the box and to come up with creative solutions to problems.

By teaching problem-solving skills and encouraging children to practice these skills on their own, parents can help children to develop the skills they need to manage their emotions and navigate difficult situations.

- **Encouraging independence**: Allowing children to make their own decisions and solve problems on their own can help them to develop self-sufficiency and independence. Parents can encourage independence by giving children age-appropriate responsibilities and allowing them to make their own decisions within limits. Encouraging independence is an important part of helping children to develop self-sufficiency and to become more confident and capable. Independence involves the ability to make decisions and solve problems on one's own. Parents can encourage independence by giving children age-appropriate responsibilities and allowing them to make their own decisions within limits. This can involve allowing children to make decisions about their own activities and responsibilities, such as choosing their own clothes or planning their own free time. It can also involve giving children the opportunity to solve problems on their own and to take on new challenges and responsibilities. By encouraging independence, parents can help children to develop their decision-making skills and to become more self-sufficient and confident.

By providing support and guidance and helping children to develop the skills they need to manage their emotions and navigate challenges, parents can strengthen the parent-child connection and help their children to grow and develop.

Spending special time with children, listening to them, and validating their feelings are all important ways to create a strong connection with them. Other ways to strengthen the parent-child connection include sharing your own feelings and thoughts when appropriate, focusing on solutions with children after a cooling-off period, and asking curiosity questions to help children explore the consequences of their choices. Hugs can also be a powerful way to show love and support. When children feel a strong connection with their parents, they are more likely to feel a sense of belonging and significance, and this can help to reduce misbehavior. Using positive discipline techniques, such as family meetings or class meetings and joint problem-solving, can also be effective in creating a connection with children and involving them in finding solutions. These techniques involve respect and collaboration and can help children to feel heard and valued.

BUILDING A SAFE AND SUPPORTIVE ENVIRONMENT

It is important for parents to create a safe and supportive environment for their children, and to make use of times when there is less distress or anxiety to build the parent-child connection. Spending special time with children and enjoying their company is a great way to strengthen the bond between parents and children. Parents can also have talks with children that focus on solutions to problems and ask curiosity questions to help children explore the consequences of their choices. These types of interactions can help children to feel heard and valued and can encourage them to develop their decision-making skills and emotional intelligence. By creating a supportive and positive environment and building a strong connection with their children, parents can help their children to feel confident and capable, and to navigate challenges and difficult situations more effectively. Some additional strategies include:

- **Being present and available**: This involves making time for your children and giving them your full attention when they need it. This means setting aside distractions such as phones or other screens and giving your children your full attention. When children feel that their parents are present and available for them, they are more likely to feel a sense of connection and support. This can be especially important during times of stress or difficulty, when children may need extra attention and support. By being present and available for your children, you can show them that you value and care about them and that you are there to support them.

- **Providing emotional support**: This involves showing empathy and understanding, and offering comfort and reassurance when children are upset. When children are upset or distressed, they often need someone to listen to their feelings and offer support. By showing empathy and understanding, and offering comfort and reassurance, parents can help children to feel heard and valued, and cope with their emotions in a healthy way. This can involve listening to children's feelings and helping them to express themselves, offering a hug or physical touch to show support and reassuring children that they are loved and valued. By providing emotional support, parents can help their children to feel more connected and supported, and to navigate challenges and difficult situations more effectively.

- **Encouraging open communication**: This involves creating an open and accepting environment where children feel comfortable talking about their thoughts and feelings. When children feel that their parents are open and accepting, they are more likely to feel comfortable sharing their thoughts and feelings, which can help to strengthen the parent-child bond. Some ways that parents can encourage open communication include:

- **Asking open-ended questions**: This can involve asking questions that encourage children to share their thoughts and feelings, such as "How did you feel when that happened?" or "What are you thinking about right now?"

- **Listening actively**: This involves giving children your full attention when they are speaking and showing that you are interested in what they have to say.

- **Validating and acknowledging emotions**: This involves acknowledging and understanding the emotions that children are experiencing and letting them know that their feelings are valid and normal.

- **Avoiding judgment or criticism**: This involves being accepting and non-judgmental when children share their thoughts and feelings and avoiding criticism or judgment. By encouraging open communication and creating an open and accepting environment, parents can help their children to feel comfortable sharing their thoughts and feelings and build a stronger connection with them.

- **Teaching coping skills**: This involves helping children to develop strategies for managing their emotions and coping with stress, such as deep breathing, counting to ten, or using positive self-talk.

- **Encouraging independence**: This involves giving children age-appropriate responsibilities and allowing them to make their own decisions within limits, which can help them to develop self-sufficiency and independence. Independence involves the ability to make decisions and solve problems on one's own. Parents can encourage independence by giving children age-appropriate responsibilities and allowing them to make their own decisions within limits. This can involve allowing children to make decisions about their own activities and responsibilities, such as choosing their own clothes or planning their own free time. It can also involve giving children the opportunity to solve problems on their own and to take on new challenges and responsibilities. By encouraging independence, parents can help children to develop their decision-making skills and to become more self-sufficient and confident. This can also strengthen the parent-child connection, as children who feel trusted and valued are more likely to feel a strong sense of connection with their parents.

Involving children in rational discussions of their choices and behaviors is a proactive and effective way to strengthen the parent-child connection. This approach involves engaging both the heart and the rational parts of the brain, which can help children to feel heard and valued and to develop their own insights and understanding. By having honest and open talks with children about their choices and behaviors, parents can help them to understand the consequences of those actions and to develop problem-solving and decision-making skills. This approach can be more

effective than simply reacting and imposing consequences, as it involves respect and collaboration and
helps children to feel more invested in finding solutions. By involving children in rational discussions and
being proactive in addressing behaviors and challenges,
parents can strengthen the connection with their children and help them to develop the skills they need to
navigate difficult situations more effectively.

In this chapter on connection versus controlling,
parents learn that when they are too controlling, they
risk undermining their child's sense of autonomy and
self-esteem. On the other hand, when they are
connected, they create a sense of trust and understanding with their child, which leads to greater cooperation and open communication.

This chapter explores various techniques for maintaining a connected relationship with their children,
such as active listening, validation, empathy, and setting
clear, consistent boundaries. It may also discuss the
importance of understanding a child's emotional needs
and how to respond to them in a way that promotes
connection and trust.

The next chapter, "Fight or Flight," explores how
parents can respond effectively to the challenging
behaviors of their children. The chapter will discuss
how children's behavior is often a response to stress,

fear, or other underlying emotions and that a child's behavior can be a sign that they are struggling emotionally.

It covers techniques for parents to manage their own emotions in the face of their children's challenging behavior and also how to approach children when they behave in a way that is difficult, be it verbal and physical aggression, running away or getting lost, etc. It will also provide strategies for helping children to regulate their own emotions and behavior, such as deep breathing exercises, mindfulness, and other coping mechanisms.

3

FIGHT OR FLIGHT

As parents, one of the most challenging aspects of raising children is helping them to navigate the powerful emotions and behaviors that arise as a result of the world around them. In this chapter, we will delve into the workings of the limbic system, a group of brain structures located in the center of the brain that are responsible for regulating emotions and behavior. We will focus on the fight or flight response, a natural reaction to perceived threats or danger that can play a major role in shaping the way children react to stress and adversity.

The limbic system contains structures such as the amygdala, responsible for the processing of emotions such as fear and aggression, and the hippocampus, involved in memory and emotion regulation. When the body is faced with a perceived threat, the amygdala sends a signal to the hypothalamus, activating the sympathetic nervous system and releasing stress hormones, which triggers the fight-or-flight response, including an increase in heart rate, blood pressure, and breathing rate, and a release of energy to the muscles.

In this chapter, we'll discuss the impact of this response on children, how it can manifest in different ways, and practical strategies for parents to help children manage these emotions and behaviors. From understanding how the limbic system works to providing emotional support and teaching coping mechanisms, we'll explore ways to help children develop resilience and emotional intelligence. This chapter is an important step in understanding how to help children navigate their emotions and respond to the world around them in a healthy way.

WHAT IS THE LIMBIC SYSTEM?

The limbic system is a group of brain structures that are located in the center of the brain and are involved in the regulation of emotions and behavior. The limbic system contains the amygdala, which is responsible for the processing of emotions such as fear and aggression. It also contains the hippocampus, which is involved in the consolidation of new memories and the regulation of emotions. The limbic system plays a key role in the body's fight-or-flight response, which is a natural response to threats or danger which prepares the body for action. When the body is faced with a perceived threat, the amygdala sends a signal to the hypothalamus, which activates the sympathetic nervous system and causes the release of stress hormones. These hormones trigger the body's fight-or-flight response, which can include an increase in heart rate, blood pressure, and breathing rate, and a release of energy to the muscles. The limbic system is an important part of the human brain that plays a key role in regulating emotions and behavior.

It is common for children to have strong emotional reactions when faced with limits or boundaries. This can include tantrums, crying, and other negative behaviors. It is important for parents to remember that these reactions are a normal part of child development and do not necessarily reflect poorly on their parenting skills. When children are faced with limits or boundaries, they may feel frustrated, angry, or powerless, and may act out in negative ways as a result. It is important for parents to recognize that these reactions are a normal part of child development and to respond in a way that is supportive and understanding. This may involve acknowledging the child's feelings and helping them to find appropriate ways to express their emotions. It can also involve setting clear and consistent limits and boundaries and helping children to understand the reasons behind those limits. By viewing tantrums and other negative behaviors as a normal part of child development and responding in a supportive and understanding way, parents can help their children to develop healthy coping skills and to manage their emotions in a healthy way.

It is also common for children to experience strong emotional ups and downs, and it can be confusing and frustrating for parents when a child who was happy and loving one moment becomes upset and emotional over a seemingly insignificant issue. There are several reasons why this can happen. One reason is that children are still developing their emotional regulation skills, and they may struggle to manage their emotions at times. Another reason is that children are often more sensitive to stress and change than adults, and even small events or transitions can trigger strong emotional reactions. Additionally, children may have a hard time communicating their needs and feelings and may act out or become upset when they feel overwhelmed or frustrated. It is important for parents to remember that children are still learning how to manage their emotions and respond in a supportive and under-standing way when their child is upset. This may involve acknowledging their feelings and helping them to find healthy ways to cope with their emotions.

Emotions play a significant role in children's lives and can have a powerful influence on their thoughts, behaviors, and relationships. Understanding how a child's feelings come about can be an important part of parenting, as it can help parents to better understand their child's needs and to provide the support and guidance they need. Some factors that can contribute to a child's emotional state include: their experiences and environment, their relationships and social connections, and their physical and mental health. By learning about these factors and paying attention to their child's emotional needs, parents can provide the support and guidance that is necessary for their child's emotional well-being. This can involve listening to their child's feelings and concerns, providing emotional support and comfort, and helping them to develop healthy coping skills. By understanding and supporting their child's emotions, parents can play a vital role in their child's development and well-being.

It's certainly true that when we are caught up in the midst of strong emotions, it can be difficult to think clearly and to engage in logical, rational thinking. It's natural to feel upset and frustrated in these situations, and it can be difficult to make sense of things. However, it is still important to try to approach the situation with as much calm and clarity as possible, even if it is challenging. This can help us to better understand the situation and to find ways to resolve it effectively. It might be helpful to take a step back, take some deep breaths, and try to clear your mind before attempting to engage in any problem-solving or communication.

It's incredibly helpful to have an understanding of how our brains and bodies respond to stress and emotions. When we are faced with a challenging situation, our bodies respond by releasing stress hormones like cortisol and adrenaline. These hormones can affect our thinking and behavior and can make it more difficult to think clearly and to make good decisions. It's important to remember that when someone is behaving in an emotional or irrational way, it may be because they are feeling overwhelmed or stressed. This can be especially true if the person is already prone to anxiety or other emotional issues.

It can also be very helpful to try to take a step back and consider what might be causing the person's emotional response. Are they under a lot of stress? Are they dealing with personal problems? Understanding the root cause of their behavior can help you to respond in a more compassionate and understanding way, and may even help you to find ways to support them and help them to manage their emotions more effectively.

It's true that when a child is experiencing strong emotions, it can be difficult for them to think clearly and regulate their behavior. The stress response that you describe, which involves the release of stress hormones and the activation of the amygdala and hypothalamus, can affect a child's ability to think rationally and control their actions. It's important to remember that when a child is behaving in an emotional or irrational way, it may not be because they are being difficult on purpose. They may be feeling overwhelmed or threatened, and may not have the capacity to regulate their emotions effectively in the moment.

In situations like this, it can be helpful to try to remain calm and provide the child with emotional support. This might involve simply being present with the child and offering a comforting presence, or it could involve helping the child to identify and express their feelings. It can also be helpful to provide the child with a sense of structure and routine, as this can help them to feel more secure and more able to manage their emotions. Ultimately, the key is to be patient and understanding and to try to help the child to feel safe and supported as they learn to cope with their emotions.

The prefrontal cortex is a region of the brain that plays a key role in higher cognitive functions such as planning, decision-making, and impulse control. It is one of the last areas of the brain to fully develop, and this process continues into the mid-20s in humans. Inhibition and impulse control are complex functions that are mediated by the prefrontal cortex, and they are still developing among adolescents and young adults. This can make it more difficult for people in this age group to regulate their behavior and make good decisions, particularly in situations where they are under stress or experiencing strong emotions.

It's important to try to regulate your own emotions before trying to help your child manage their emotions. When we are upset or stressed, it can be difficult to think clearly and respond in a helpful way. Taking a few deep breaths or finding a way to calm down can make a big difference in how you approach the situation. If you're feeling overwhelmed, it's also a good idea to step back and ask for help if you need it. This could be as simple as asking your partner to take over for a little while or confiding in a friend or family member. Remember that it's okay to take care of yourself and prioritize your own well-being in order to be there for your child.

MIRROR NEURONS

Mirror neurons are a type of brain cell that is thought to play a role in how we understand and interact with other people. When we observe someone else performing an action, such as running or smiling, the same brain regions that are involved in performing that action ourselves are activated. This may help us to understand what other people are feeling and to respond in a way that is appropriate for the situation.

Research on mirror neurons in children is still limited, but what we do know suggests that these cells may be important for helping kids to learn and understand the actions and emotions of others. For example, it's thought that mirror neurons may be involved in the way that babies and young children learn to imitate the actions and expressions of the people around them. By observing and copying the behavior of others, they can learn about social norms and appropriate ways of behaving.

So, when a parent is able to regulate their own emotions and behaviors, it may have a positive influence on their child through the activation of mirror neurons. This is just one possible mechanism, and more research is needed to fully understand how this process works.

CALMING THE SITUATION

When a child is upset, it's important for the parent or caregiver to remain calm and to use nonverbal cues to communicate warmth and empathy. This can help to signal to the child that they are safe and that there is no danger, which can help to reduce the child's stress and anxiety. Nonverbal cues such as maintaining eye contact, crouching down to the child's level, and using a calm and empathic tone of voice can all be effective in conveying a sense of understanding and support. It's also important to focus more on actions rather than words, as children are often more attuned to nonverbal cues and can be more influenced by them.

Different children have different preferences when it comes to physical touch and affection, and it's important for parents to be mindful of this. Some children may find physical touch from a parent very comforting and reassuring during times of distress, while others may find it overwhelming or even aversive. It's important to pay attention to your child's cues and to respect their boundaries when it comes to physical affection. If your child seems to be receptive to physical touch, you might try offering a hug or gentle pat on the back as a way of providing comfort and support. However, if your child seems to be overwhelmed by physical touch, it's important to respect their wishes and find other ways to offer support and comfort.

It can be helpful to teach children coping skills that they can use to self-soothe and regulate their emotions when they are upset. This can be especially useful for children who are prone to tantrums or emotional outbursts. There are many different types of activities and techniques that can be helpful for calming the body and mind, and it's often a good idea to try out a few different options to see what works best for your child.

Some ideas for calming sensory inputs include: Fidget spinners or other small, handheld toys that can be manipulated with the fingers silly putty or other soft, pliable materials that can be squeezed and molded, pushed, or pressed on a wall or other firm surface, taking slow, deep breaths, listening to calming music or white noise, doing a simple stretching or relaxation exercise. It's important to try to introduce these coping skills before a meltdown occurs so that your child has the opportunity to practice and become familiar with them. This can help them to feel more confident and capable of managing their emotions on their own when they are upset.

When a child is highly emotional or upset, it is often not the best time to try to teach or explain things to them. This is because their brain is in a heightened state of arousal, and they may not be able to think clearly or process new information. It's better to wait until the child has calmed down and their prefrontal cortex is functioning more normally before trying to have a conversation about what happened.

THE CALM AFTER THE STORM

Once the child has had a chance to calm down, it can be helpful to help them reflect on the situation and "form a story" about what happened. This means helping them to understand and make sense of their emotions and the events that led up to the meltdown. This can be a valuable learning opportunity for the child, as it can help them to develop the skills of emotional self-regulation and problem-solving. It's important to be patient and to approach this conversation with empathy and understanding, rather than blame or criticism.

It's natural for young children to want to test limits and push against boundaries, and it's an important part of their development. However, it's also important for parents to be firm and consistent in setting and enforcing limits, as this helps children to learn self-control and to understand the rules and expectations of their environment.

When a child has a tantrum or becomes upset because a limit has been set, it can be helpful to remember that the child is probably feeling frustrated and disappointed because they are unable to have what they want. It's important to be patient and to recognize that this is a normal part of childhood development. By approaching the situation with empathy and understanding, and helping the child to express and cope with their emotions, you can help them to learn how to regulate their behavior and understand that they cannot always have what they want.

When a child is upset or having a tantrum, it's important for the parent or caregiver to remain calm and to provide a supportive and accepting environment. This can help the child to feel safe and understood, which can make it easier for them to regulate their emotions and behavior.

It's not always necessary or even possible to understand exactly what the child is upset about, and it's often more helpful to focus on the child's emotions rather than trying to identify the specific cause of the upset. By staying present and supportive, you can help the child to feel seen and heard, and learn how to cope with strong emotions in a healthy and constructive way. This can be challenging at times, but it's an important part of helping children to develop emotional intelligence and self-regulation skills.

It's important to try to stay present and focused when your child is upset and to provide a supportive and accepting environment. This can help the child to feel safe and understood, and to know that their feelings and emotions are accepted by the adults in their life. This can be a very powerful message for a child, as it helps them to feel valued and supported and to develop trust in their relationships.

It can be helpful to have a "go-to" strategy or technique that you can use when your child is upset, such as taking deep breaths together or using a comfort object. However, it's also important to be flexible and to adapt your approach to the needs of the child in each specific situation. Consistency is key, but it's also important to be responsive and to adjust your approach as needed in order to best meet the needs of your child.

When you have found the technique to calm your child after a tantrum, you should continue to stick to this technique. Consistency in your method will be the best way to keep your chosen calming technique as a safe space for your child. The fight-or-flight reflex can seem impossible to break through, but it can always be made more manageable when you find a method that works for your family. If you have an older child who is able to effectively communicate their needs with you after a tantrum, then you can try to ask them what you can do better to work through these difficult moments. Often a very young child will not know, but sometimes a slightly older child might be able to give you a little guidance on what they need.

The moments after a tantrum are a fantastic opportunity for you to reflect with your child. These moments during the calming process can be key to connecting effectively with your child in emotional situations. The post-tantrum emotions your child might feel can easily be transferable into emotions they will feel as they grow older so as parents, we can offer the chance for a child to develop healthy coping skills to better handle emotions into adulthood. Meaningful connections between parents and their children are sometimes the most vital part of developing a healthy relationship between family members when those children are teenagers. It also models healthy relationships so when your child moves into adulthood they are able to strive to form their own healthy friendships and relationships.

Even when it seems tough and the tantrums feel endless just keep going. Take the chance to calm down whenever you can and don't feel afraid of removing yourself from the situation when necessary. During these tantrums just know you are doing what is best for your child and shut out any outside judgment.

In this chapter "Fight or Flight," parents have learned how to respond effectively to their children's challenging behaviors. This chapter has covered how to manage their own emotions in the face of their children's challenging behavior, and how to approach children when they behave in a way that is difficult, be it verbal and physical aggression, running away or getting lost, etc. It also provides strategies for helping children to regulate their own emotions and behavior, such as deep breathing exercises, mindfulness, and other coping mechanisms.

This chapter has also explored how to differentiate between challenging behaviors that require a disciplinary response and those that are a sign that a child is struggling emotionally. It has emphasized the importance of recognizing the underlying emotions that drive the behavior and responding in a way that helps the child feel safe and supported.

The next chapter in the book is to stay with them closely and it continues the theme of building a strong and healthy relationship with your child. The next chapter will discuss the importance of maintaining a strong bond with your child as they grow and develop, and how to balance the natural pull of independence with the need for connection. It will also explore the ways in which parents can stay connected with their children throughout their different stages of development, such as through quality time, open communication, shared activities, and emotional support. The chapter will also cover some of the challenges to staying connected, and how parents can address them.

4

STAY WITH THEM CLOSELY

As parents, one of the most important things we can do for our children is to provide emotional support during difficult times. Whether it's a small disappointment or a major crisis, children rely on their parents to be a steady and comforting presence in their lives. In this chapter, we will explore different strategies for staying close with your child and providing emotional support during highly charged or emotional moments.

It's natural to want to fix problems or make our children feel better immediately, but it's important to remember that sometimes the best thing we can do is simply be present and offer comfort and support. Some things you can try to provide emotional support to your child during a difficult time include staying close and maintaining physical contact, using a warm and comforting tone of voice, validating the child's feelings and acknowledging their emotions, offering comfort and reassurance, helping the child to find words to describe their feelings, and providing a safe and supportive environment for the child to express their emotions.

It's important to remember that each child is unique, and what works for one child may not work for another. It's important to be flexible and to adapt your approach to the needs and preferences of your child.

This chapter will provide you with practical strategies for staying close and providing emotional support for your child during difficult times. By following these strategies, you can help your child to feel safe and supported, and to develop the resilience and emotional intelligence they need to navigate the ups and downs of life.

Staying with your child and providing emotional support during a highly charged or emotional time can be challenging, but it is an important part of being a supportive and caring parent. It's natural to want to try to fix the problem or make the child feel better right away, but sometimes the most helpful thing you can do is simply be present and offer comfort and support. Some things you can try to provide emotional support to your child during a difficult time include: Staying close to the child and maintaining physical contact, if the child is receptive to it, using a warm and comforting tone of voice, validating the child's feelings and acknowledging their emotions, offering comfort and reassurance, helping the child to find words to describe their feelings, providing a safe and supportive environment for the child to express their emotions. It's important to remember that each child is unique, and what works for one child may not work for another. It's a good idea to be flexible and to adapt your approach to the needs and preferences of your child.

Staying and listening to your child when they are upset can be a very powerful way to provide emotional support and comfort. When a child is crying, having a tantrum, or experiencing fear, it's natural for them to feel overwhelmed and unsure of what to do. By staying with them and listening to them, you can help them to feel heard and understood, and to know that you are there for them.

Saying "It's okay" or similar phrases can be a helpful way to convey understanding and support, as long as it is done in a sincere and comforting way. It's important to remember that each child is unique, and what works for one child may not work for another. It's a good idea to be flexible and to adapt your approach to the needs and preferences of your child.

When a child is upset or experiencing a problem, it's important to be supportive and understanding, rather than lecturing or criticizing. This approach can help the child feel heard and validated, and it allows them the space and freedom to work through their emotions and find their own solutions. It's important to remember that children are learning and growing, and they will make mistakes and have challenges along the way. By being a supportive and understanding parent, you can help your child feel loved and supported as they navigate these challenges and learn from them.

THE IMPORTANCE OF CRYING

It's natural for children (and adults) to feel upset and emotional at times, and crying can be a healthy way to release those emotions. When a child is crying, it's important to be there for them, offer comfort and support, and let them know that it's okay to feel their emotions. But it's also important to give them the space and freedom to work through those emotions on their own, rather than trying to fix the problem for them or stopping the crying. This can allow the child to process and deal with their emotions in a healthy way, and can ultimately lead to a sense of resolution and calm. It's also important to remember that each child is different, and some may need more comfort and support than others. It's important to be attuned to your child's needs and respond in a way that feels supportive and appropriate for them.

It's important for parents to recognize that crying is a natural and healthy way for children (and adults) to express their emotions. While it can be challenging to see our children upset or in distress, it's important to allow them to experience and express their emotions, rather than trying to suppress or discourage them. By encouraging children to express their emotions, we can help them learn to cope with and manage their emotions in a healthy way. This can ultimately lead to more emotionally healthy and resilient children. If you have a history of being discouraged from crying as a child, it may be helpful to work with a therapist or other mental health professional to explore and understand the impact this may have had on your emotional well-being. They can help you develop healthy coping strategies and work through any emotions that may have been suppressed in the past.

It's definitely challenging to be a parent, and it can be especially difficult when our children are upset or have a tantrum in public. It's natural to want to do whatever we can to stop the crying or tantrum as quickly as possible, especially if we feel like we are being judged or watched by others. But it's important to remember that children's emotions can be intense and over-whelming, and they may not have the ability to regulate them or stop crying on command. In these situations, it can be helpful to try to remain calm and offer comfort and support to your child, rather than becoming upset or frustrated yourself. This can help your child feel validated and supported, and can ultimately help them calm down more quickly. It's also important to remember that it's okay to take a break and remove yourself and your child from the situation if you need to. It's better to give your child the space and time they need to work through their emotions, rather than trying to force them to stop crying or having a tantrum.

When children are upset or experiencing a problem, it can be tempting to try to fix the problem or stop the crying as quickly as possible. However, it's important to remember that children's emotions can be intense and overwhelming, and they may not have the ability to regulate them or stop crying on command. In these situations, it's important to be patient and under-standing and to offer comfort and support to your child. This can help your child feel heard and validated, and it allows them the space and freedom to work through their emotions and find their own solutions.

It's also important to remember that children are learning and growing, and they will make mistakes and have challenges along the way. By being a supportive and understanding parent, you can help your child feel loved and supported as they navigate these challenges and learn from them. This can ultimately lead to more emotionally healthy and resilient children.

It's true that babies are born with the ability to express and process their emotions. Crying is one way that babies communicate their needs and emotions, and it's an important part of their development. However, as children grow and develop, they may learn to suppress or avoid expressing their emotions, either because they have been taught to do so or because they have not had the opportunity to practice expressing and processing their emotions in a healthy way.

It's important for parents to recognize the importance of nurturing and encouraging their children's emotional expression. By allowing children to express and process their emotions in a healthy way, parents can help them develop the skills they need to cope with and manage their emotions throughout their lives. This can ultimately lead to more emotionally healthy and resilient children.

It's also important for parents to model healthy emotional expressions for their children. By expressing and processing our own emotions in a healthy way, we can teach our children that it's okay to have and express emotions and that it's an important part of being a healthy, well-adjusted person.

It's vital for parents to recognize that it's not their job to toughen up their children or protect them from experiencing difficult emotions. In fact, it's quite the opposite. By being present and supportive when our children are experiencing painful emotions, we can help them feel safe and supported as they work through and process those emotions. This can ultimately lead to more emotionally healthy and resilient children.

You're correct if you think that in the beginning, it may seem like your child's crying is getting worse when you offer comfort and support. This is because your child may be feeling safe enough to fully express and release their emotions, and the crying may be a way for them to process and cope with those emotions. Crying is indeed a natural and healthy way for the body to regulate and cope with emotions, and it's an important part of the emotional processing and healing process.

It's important to be patient and understanding during these times and to offer comfort and support to your child. This can help your child feel heard and validated, and it allows them the space and freedom to work through their emotions and find their own solutions.

It's also important to remember that each child is different, and some may need more comfort and support than others. It's important to be attuned to your child's needs and respond in a way that feels supportive and appropriate for them.

LEARNING TO SELF-REGULATE

Regulation is an important part of emotional health and well-being, and it's something that children are still learning and developing as they grow and mature. When children are upset or experiencing a problem, it's often because they are feeling dysregulated or out of balance. It's natural for parents to want to understand what is causing their child's upset, but it's important to remember that children's emotions can be intense and overwhelming, and they may not have the ability to explain what is causing their upset.

In these situations, it can be helpful to offer comfort and support to your child, rather than trying to under-stand or fix the problem. By bringing your total presence to your child, you can help your child feel heard and validated, and you can offer them the support they need to work through their emotions and find their own solutions. Limbic resonance is a powerful tool that can help your child feel safe and supported as they work through their emotions, and it can ultimately help them regulate their emotions and find a sense of balance and calm.

It's important for parents to recognize the importance of being present and supportive when their children are upset or experiencing emotions. By being there for your child and offering comfort and support, you can help your child feel heard and validated, and you can offer them the support they need to work through their emotions and find their own solutions. This can ultimately lead to more emotionally healthy and resilient children.

It's also important to remember that once your child has returned to a state of regulation, it's appropriate to discuss boundaries and consequences and teach them tangible skills that they can use to cope with their emotions. This can help your child learn to manage their emotions in a healthy way and can ultimately lead to more emotionally healthy and resilient children.

It's okay if you have made mistakes in the past and withheld your love or support when your child was upset. It's important to recognize these mistakes and to make an effort to do better in the future. By being present and supportive when your child is upset, you can help your child feel loved and valued, and you can teach them the importance of emotional expression and vulnerability. It's never too late to start again and make positive changes in your parenting approach.

It's true that our parenting style and the way we respond to our children's emotions can be influenced by our own emotional experiences and history. If we don't know how to show up with curiosity and compassion for our children when they are upset, it may be because we have not learned how to do this for ourselves. This is completely normal, and it's something that can be learned and developed with time and practice.

Holding space for your children's big emotions is an important parenting skill, and it's something that can have a lasting impact on your child's emotional well-being and resilience. By being present and supportive when your child is upset, you can help your child feel heard and validated, and you can offer them the support they need to work through their emotions and find their own solutions. This can ultimately lead to more emotionally healthy and resilient children.

It's important to remember that our children don't just need activities, sports, vacations, and toys to be happy and fulfilled. They also need the opportunity to express and process their emotions in a healthy way, and to learn how to cope with and manage their emotions. If children cannot process their emotions, they may have difficulty enjoying life's pleasures and may struggle to cope with challenges and setbacks. By being a supportive and understanding parent, you can help your child develop the skills they need to navigate the ups and downs of life with confidence and resilience.

It's also important for parents to prioritize their own physical, emotional, and spiritual needs in order to be able to respond with love, curiosity, and compassion to their children when they are in distress. Emotional regulation is an important part of this process, and it involves taking responsibility for our own feelings and needs and being mindful of how our emotions and physical well-being impact our ability to parent from a calm and loving space.

It's okay to prioritize your own needs and to make time for self-care in order to be able to be present and supportive of your children. In fact, this is an important part of being a healthy and effective parent. By taking care of yourself, you can model healthy self-care for your children, and you can teach them the importance of taking care of themselves as well. This might mean making time for exercise, meditation, or other activities that nourish your mind and body, or seeking professional support if you need it.

It's good to remember that children learn by watching and observing their parents, and they will often model their own behaviors and habits after what they see and experience in their homes. By being mindful of your own needs and taking care of yourself, you can teach your children important lessons about self-care and emotional regulation, and you can set a positive example for them to follow.

It's common for people to have difficulty managing and coping with their emotions, especially if they have not had the opportunity to learn healthy ways of expressing and processing their emotions. If you are struggling with this, know that you are not alone and that there are resources available to help you.

It may be helpful to seek support from a therapist or other mental health professional, who can help you explore and understand your emotions, and develop healthy coping strategies for managing them. You can also try practicing mindfulness, which involves bringing your attention to the present moment and your experience in a non-judgmental way. This can help you become more aware of your emotions and can ultimately help you manage them more effectively.

Remember, it's never too late to learn and grow, and it's always possible to improve your emotional well-being and resilience. Don't be afraid to reach out for support and make your own emotional well-being a priority.

EYE CONTACT

Maintaining eye contact with your child can be an important part of staying connected and engaged with them, especially during times when they are upset or acting out. Eye contact can help your child feel seen and heard, and it can help establish and strengthen your emotional connection.

It's natural for parents to want to do whatever they can to calm their child during a temper tantrum, but it's important to remember that sometimes the best approach is to simply withstand the tantrum and offer comfort and support. This can be challenging, especially in the heat of the moment, but it's an important part of helping your child work through their emotions and find a sense of resolution and calm.

It can be helpful to focus on being comforting and calm, even if it feels impossible at times. This can help your child feel more secure and supported, and it can ultimately help them regulate their emotions and find a sense of balance and calm. It's also important to remember that each child is different, and some may need more comfort and support than others. It's important to be attuned to your child's needs and to respond in a way that feels supportive and appropriate for them.

It's true that eye contact can establish and strengthen emotional connections, and it's an important part of building and maintaining relationships. From birth, babies are programmed to make eye contact with their mothers, and this helps establish a strong emotional bond between them. When a mother engages in eye contact with her feeding baby, it helps facilitate communication and strengthen the emotional connection between them.

Oxytocin, the hormone of nurturing and connection, plays a role in this process, and it has many health benefits for both infants and adults. Oxytocin can help lower levels of stress, pain, and inflammation, and it can help regulate heart rate and breathing. It's also been associated with feelings of love, trust, and bonding, and it can have a positive impact on social and emotional well-being.

Maintaining eye contact and engaging in other behaviors that facilitate emotional connection can be an important part of building and maintaining healthy, supportive relationships, and it can have a positive impact on overall well-being and happiness.

It's true that many parenting strategies, such as scolding, time-outs, or offering rewards or treats, may not be effective in helping children cope with their emotions and may even contribute to more challenging behaviors in the long run.

On the other hand, staying close and listening to your child's natural instinct to cry, scream, or have tantrums can be an effective way of helping them work through their emotions and find a resolution. When you offer support and validation to your child, it helps them feel heard and understood, and it can ultimately help them feel more secure and supported. This can lead to a number of positive outcomes, including better sleep and eating habits, increased patience and resilience, and fewer daily disputes and conflicts.

It's also important to recognize that some behaviors, such as tantrums or crying, may be a natural part of the healing process, and that staying close and listening can help your child work through their emotions and find a resolution. This can ultimately help your child develop the skills they need to cope with challenges and setbacks, and to bounce back after a difficult experience. By approaching your child with an open heart and staying close and listening, you can help your child develop resilience and emotional well-being.

In this chapter, parents have learned about the importance of maintaining a strong bond with their children as they grow and develop. The chapter has covered ways to balance the natural pull of independence with the need for connection, such as quality time, open communication, shared activities, and emotional support. It has also explored some of the challenges to staying connected and how parents can address them.

The next chapter in the book builds upon the previous chapter by discussing the pitfalls of lecturing and the benefits of alternative forms of communication. The next chapter will explore the reasons why lecturing is ineffective and may even be counterproductive in many situations, and will explore the alternative methods that can be more effective. It will also discuss how to give instructions and feedback that are clear and constructive, rather than critical or judgmental, and how to encourage children to take responsibility for their own learning and behavior. The following chapter will also suggest examples of activities and exercises that can help parents to practice these alternative forms of communication.

5

DO NOT LECTURE

I t can be easy to fall into the trap of lecturing our children when they're upset or behaving in ways we don't approve of. We want to help them understand the situation and make better choices, but sometimes our well-intentioned words fall on deaf ears. In this chapter, we will explore why lecturing is often an ineffective approach when dealing with children in difficult or emotional situations, and provide alternative strategies for helping them through it.

One key factor to consider is the impact of the limbic system on children's ability to process information and think rationally when upset. The limbic system, which is responsible for emotions and behaviors, tends to take over when a person is upset, and the prefrontal cortex, which is responsible for reasoning and decision-making, can become less active. In these situations, it's important to first help the child regulate their emotions before trying to address the issue at hand. This might involve simply acknowledging the child's feelings and providing comfort and support. Once the child has calmed down, it may be easier to have a productive conversation and work toward a resolution.

We will explore strategies such as this in this chapter, in addition to providing guidance on how to respond more effectively when children are upset or behaving in challenging ways. We will also discuss how to manage one's own frustration and offer reminders to be patient and to remember that it's normal for children to have strong emotions and to need support in regulating them. With the guidance of this chapter, you will have a better understanding of how to approach and manage difficult situations with your child and support them in a more effective way.

When a child is upset, it can be difficult for them to process information and engage in rational thinking. The limbic system, which is responsible for emotions and behaviors, tends to take over when a person is upset, and the prefrontal cortex, which is responsible for reasoning and decision-making, can become less active. In these situations, it's important to first help the child regulate their emotions before trying to address the issue at hand. This might involve simply acknowledging the child's feelings and providing comfort and support. Once the child has calmed down, it may be easier to have a productive conversation and work toward a resolution.

When a child is upset, it can be challenging for a parent to know how to best support them. It can be frustrating when the strategies that we normally rely on don't seem to be effective, and it's natural to feel at a loss in these situations. However, it's important to remember that every child is different, and what works for one child may not work for another. It's okay to try different approaches and to seek guidance from others, such as a pediatrician or a child therapist if you're struggling to support your child. It's also important to be patient and to remember that it's normal for children to have strong emotions and to need support in regulating them. With time and practice, you will likely find approaches that are effective in helping your child through difficult times.

APPRECIATE OUR DIFFERENCES

It's important to remember that every child is different, and what works for one child may not work for another. In these situations, it can be helpful to focus on helping the child regulate their emotions first. This might involve acknowledging their feelings and providing comfort and support. Once the child has calmed down, it may be easier to have a productive conversation and work toward a resolution. It's also important to be patient and to remember that it's normal for children to have strong emotions and to need support in regulating them. It can be helpful to try different approaches and to seek guidance from others, such as a pediatrician or a child therapist if you're struggling to support your child. With time and practice, you will likely find approaches that are effective in helping your child through difficult times.

Listening and providing nonverbal signs of warmth and attentiveness can be helpful in supporting a child who is upset. When a child is upset, their limbic system, which is responsible for emotions and behaviors, tends to be more active. By providing nonverbal signs of warmth and attentiveness, such as making eye contact, nodding, and using a calm and caring tone of voice, you can help the child feel heard and understood, which can in turn help to regulate their emotions. This can create a more positive and constructive environment in which you can have a productive conversation and work towards a resolution. It's important to remember, however, that every child is different and may respond differently to different approaches. It's okay to try different strategies and to seek guidance from others if you're struggling to support your child.

LESS IS MORE

Sometimes, less is more when it comes to interacting with kids. While it's important to be involved in your child's life and to set boundaries and expectations, it's also important to be mindful of how you communicate with them. Lecturing can sometimes be counterproductive, as it can make a child feel unheard and misunderstood, and may not necessarily lead to a positive resolution. It's important to remember that when a child is upset, their limbic system, which is responsible for emotions and behaviors, tends to be more active, and the prefrontal cortex, which is responsible for reasoning and decision-making, can become less active. In these situations, it can be more effective to focus on acknowledging the child's feelings and providing comfort and support, rather than lecturing or trying to reason with them. It's also important to be aware of the child's individual needs and preferences, as every child is different and may respond differently to different approaches.

It's common for children to tune out or become resistant when they are lectured, especially if they feel unheard or misunderstood. It's important to be aware of the child's individual needs and preferences and to try to approach the situation in a way that takes their perspective into account. Acknowledging the child's feelings and providing comfort and support can be more effective in helping the child regulate their emotions and engage in productive problem-solving. It's also important to be patient and to remember that it's normal for children to make mistakes and to need guidance in learning how to make good choices. With time and practice, you will likely find approaches that are effective in helping your child learn and grow.

It's common for parents to lecture their children when they feel frustrated or concerned about their behavior. Lecturing can be a way for parents to try to teach their children right from wrong and to guide their behavior. However, as I mentioned earlier, lecturing can sometimes be counter-productive, as it can make a child feel unheard and misunderstood, and may not necessarily lead to a positive resolution. It's important for parents to be aware of the child's individual needs and preferences, and to try to approach the situation in a way that takes their perspective into account. With time and practice, you will likely find approaches that are effective in helping your child learn and grow.

It's true that some parents may lecture their children as a way to try to teach them right from wrong or to express their frustration or disappointment. It's also possible that some parents may lecture out of fear, as you mentioned, either because they are concerned about their child making bad choices or because they want to help their child become responsible and independent. However, it's important to remember that lecturing is not always the most effective way to teach a child or address a behavior issue. As I mentioned earlier, lecturing can sometimes be counter-productive, as it can make a child feel unheard and misunderstood, and may not necessarily lead to a positive resolution. It's important for parents to be aware of the child's individual needs and preferences, and to try to approach the situation in a way that takes their perspective into account. It's also important to be patient and to remember that it's normal for children to make mistakes and to need guidance in learning how to make good choices. With time and practice, you will likely find approaches that are effective in helping your child learn and grow.

HOW TO STOP LECTURING

It's important for parents to be mindful of how they communicate with their children, as the way we talk with them can have a big impact on our relationships and on their development. If you find that you are doing a lot of reminding, talking without listening, nagging, or using threats, it may be worth considering whether these approaches are effective in helping your child learn and grow. While it's natural for parents to want to guide and support their children, it's important to remember that children are more likely to be receptive to guidance and direction when they feel heard and understood, and when they are given the opportunity to participate in problem-solving and decision-making. It's also important to be aware of the child's individual needs and preferences and to try to approach the situation in a way that takes their perspective into account. With time and practice, you will likely find approaches that are effective in helping your child learn and grow.

Here are some additional actionable tips for how to stop lecturing kids:

- **Try to understand your child's perspective**: Take a step back and try to see things from your child's perspective. This can help you gain a better understanding of why they are behaving the way they are, and can also help you find more effective ways to address the issue.
- **Use open-ended questions**: Instead of lecturing, try asking open-ended questions that encourage your child to think and express themselves. This can help you better

understand their perspective and can also help them develop critical thinking skills.

- **Encourage problem-solving**: Instead of telling your child what to do, try to encourage them to come up with their own solutions to problems. This can help them feel more in control and can also help them develop problem-solving skills.

- **Set limits and boundaries**: It's important to set clear limits and boundaries for your child, but it's also important to do so in a way that is respectful and age-appropriate. Try to use positive language and give your child choices whenever possible.

- **Practice active listening**: Make an effort to really listen to your child when they are speaking, and show them that you are listening by making eye contact and using nonverbal cues like nodding. This can help your child feel heard and understood, which can in turn help to build trust and strengthen your relationship.

- **Seek guidance from others**: If you're struggling to break the lecturing habit or to find more effective ways to communicate with your child, it can be helpful to seek guidance from others, such as a child therapist or a parenting educator.

Remember, it's natural for parents to want to guide and support their children, and it's okay to make mistakes. With time and practice, you will likely find approaches that are effective in helping your child learn and grow.

Helping kids make a routine can be an effective way to encourage independence and self-regulation, and can also help to reduce the need for nagging and reminding. Here are some additional tips for how to help kids make a routine:

- **Start small**: If your child is new to routines, start by focusing on a few key tasks or activities. You can gradually add more tasks as your child becomes more comfortable with the routine.
- **Use visual aids**: Visual aids, such as pictures or photos, can be especially helpful for younger children who may not be able to read or understand written instructions. You can use pictures or photos of the tasks that need to be completed, or you can create a visual schedule that shows the order in which tasks should be completed.
- **Involve your child in the process**: Involving your child in the process of creating a routine can help them feel more ownership over the routine and can also help them understand the

importance of the tasks that need to be completed. You can ask your child for their input and ideas, and encourage them to take an active role in planning and organizing their routine.

- **Be consistent**: It's important to be consistent with the routine, as this can help your child learn to expect what comes next and can also help to reduce stress and anxiety. Try to follow the routine as closely as possible, and be sure to provide clear and consistent reminders when needed.

- **Be flexible**: It's okay to be flexible with the routine, especially if your child is still learning how to follow it. Be open to making adjustments as needed, and be sure to provide positive reinforcement when your child is successful in following the routine.

It's important to set clear expectations for your child and to be consistent in enforcing consequences when necessary. Here are some additional tips for how to avoid power struggles and implement consequences effectively:

- **Use clear and specific language**: Be clear and specific about what you expect your child to do, and avoid using vague or ambiguous language. Use "when-then" statements to clearly communicate the consequences that will occur if the expectation is not met. A "when-then" statement is saying something like when you finish your homework then you can go and play.

- **Avoid repeating and reminding**: It can be tempting to repeat or remind your child of their responsibilities, but this can often lead to power struggles and can be counterproductive. Instead, try to be consistent in enforcing the consequences that you have established.

- **Be firm, but fair**: It's important to be firm in enforcing consequences, but it's also important to be fair and to consider your child's perspective. Try to avoid reacting emotionally or becoming angry, and be sure to listen to your child's perspective before making a decision.

- **Stay calm**: Maintaining a calm and composed demeanor can be helpful in avoiding power struggles and in helping your child learn to regulate their emotions. Even if your child becomes upset or angry, try to stay calm and focused on the issue at hand.

- **Use positive reinforcement**: In addition to enforcing consequences, it's also important to recognize and reinforce positive behaviors and efforts. This can help your child feel motivated and supported, and can also help to build trust and strengthen your relationship.

Using short and simple words can be an effective way to communicate with children, especially younger children who may not yet have developed strong language skills. Short and simple words are easier for children to understand and can help to reduce confusion or misunderstanding. Here are some additional tips for using short words to communicate better with children:

- **Use clear and direct language**: Avoid using complex or abstract language, and instead use clear and direct language that is easy for children to understand.
- **Use simple and concrete words**: Use simple and concrete words that describe things or actions directly, rather than using more abstract or figurative language.
- **Use gestures and facial expressions**: In addition to using words, you can also use gestures and facial expressions to help communicate your message. For example, you can use a calm and caring tone of voice, and

make eye contact and smile to show that you are listening and supportive.

- **Repeat and rephrase**: If your child seems to be having trouble understanding what you are saying, try repeating the message or rephrasing it in a different way. You can also use visual aids, such as pictures or photos, to help convey your message.

- **Be patient**: Remember that children are still learning, and it may take time for them to fully understand what you are saying. Be patient and provide plenty of support and encouragement as they learn.

THE IMPORTANCE OF COMMUNICATION AND THE WORDS WE USE

Words like "never" and "always" can be particularly problematic, as they can be overly generalizing and may not accurately reflect the child's behavior. For example, saying "you never clean up your toys" or "you always forget to brush your teeth" can be frustrating for children and may lead to power struggles or resistance. Instead, try to use more specific and accurate language that describes the child's behavior in a neutral or objective way. For example, you could say, "I noticed that your toys are still scattered around the room" or "I noticed that you didn't brush your teeth this morning." This can help to avoid misunderstandings and can also help to de-escalate any tension or frustration.

Holding family meetings can be a helpful way to encourage communication and problem-solving within the family. Here are some tips for how to hold effective family meetings and ask effective questions: Set a specific time and place: Choose a time and place that is convenient for everyone and that is free of distractions. Establish ground rules for the meeting, such as taking turns speaking and listening, showing respect, and staying on topic. Identify the issue: Clearly identify the issue or concern that you want to discuss, and try to be specific and objective in your description. Encourage everyone to participate in the discussion and share their thoughts and ideas. Ask open-ended questions that encourage your child to think and express themselves, rather than asking closed-ended questions that can be answered with a simple "yes" or "no." Encourage your child to participate in problem-solving and to come up with their own solutions to the issue. After the meeting, be sure to follow up and hold everyone accountable for any action steps that were agreed upon. By holding regular family meetings and asking effective questions, you can create a safe and supportive environment for communication and problem-solving within your family.

102 | DDJ PUBLISHING

It's important to recognize that when children are upset or distressed, they may not be able to process or respond to logical reasoning or lectures in the same way that adults do. In these situations, it can be helpful to focus on making an emotional connection and providing support and understanding, rather than trying to reason with the child. This can help to calm the child's emotions and can also help to build trust and strengthen the relationship. It's also important to remember that children's brains are still developing, and they may not yet have the capacity for abstract or logical thinking. By being patient and understanding, and by providing support and guidance, you can help your child learn and grow in a healthy and positive way.

By ditching the classic boring lectures and developing a meaningful connection with your child you not only eliminate frequent emotional outbursts but you are also giving your child the chance to develop important life skills. Problem-solving, thoughtful responses, and being in tune with their own emotions are all irreplaceable skills that you will be teaching your child when you stop lecturing them. Sometimes taking a few extra minutes when leaving the house or when trying a new food at the dinner table can be all it takes to break down the problems you are facing with your child. Start to view the problems as the enemy and your child as a teammate. We often dumb things down when talking to our children but to properly establish a meaningful connection we just need to simplify our questions and give our children a safe space for them to answer us honestly. When these communication skills are built during childhood the teenage years will be a lot easier and your child is more likely to grow up as a healthy adult who is able to properly process the emotions of themselves and the people around them.

In this chapter, parents have learned about the pitfalls of lecturing and the benefits of alternative forms of communication. The chapter has explored the reasons why lecturing is ineffective and may even be counter-productive in many situations. Alternative methods that can be more effective are discussed such as clear and constructive instructions, feedback, and encouraging children to take responsibility for their own learning and behavior. It has also suggested examples of activities and exercises that can help parents to practice these alternative forms of communication.

The next chapter continues to build on the theme of effective communication with children. The chapter will discuss the difference between encouragement and praise and why one is more beneficial than the other. It will explore the impact of praise on children's self-esteem and motivation, and how encouragement can help to foster a growth mindset, self-motivation, and self-esteem. The next chapter will also provide examples of ways that parents can encourage their children and tips for making encouragement a part of daily interactions with them.

6

ENCOURAGEMENT INSTEAD OF PRAISE

As parents, we want to encourage and support our children in every aspect of their lives. We want to help them feel confident, resilient, and capable, and one way we do this is by praising their achievements and efforts. However, it's important to understand that there is a significant difference between encouragement and praise, and how we use them can have a big impact on how our children view themselves and their abilities.

This chapter will explore the difference between encouragement and praise in detail, and how to use them effectively in different situations. We will also provide practical strategies for how to encourage children in a way that helps them build confidence and resilience. Understanding the distinction and benefits of encouragement over praise will allow parents to support their children in a more effective way and help children develop a growth mindset.

WHAT IS THE DIFFERENCE BETWEEN PRAISE AND ENCOURAGEMENT?

There is a significant distinction between encouragement and praise, and it is important to understand the pros and cons of each, as well as the different benefits they can offer to children. Encouragement is a form of support that helps to motivate and inspire someone to continue or try harder. It is usually focused on the effort and progress that a person is making, rather than on their innate abilities or characteristics. Encouragement can be a powerful tool for helping children to develop resilience and a growth mindset, as it helps them to see that they can improve and succeed through their own efforts.

Praise, on the other hand, is a form of positive feedback that is typically given in recognition of someone's achievements or characteristics. Praise can be helpful in boosting confidence and self-esteem, but it can also have downsides, such as leading to a fixed mindset or a reliance on external validation. It is important to balance praise with encouragement and to focus on the specific actions and behaviors that a child is exhibiting, rather than just praising them for being "smart" or "talented."

Encouragement helps individuals to reflect on their own actions and progress, while praise may create a dependency on external approval. This can hinder personal growth and development. Therefore, using encouragement can have a more meaningful and long-lasting impact.

Encouragement involves recognizing and acknowledging an individual's efforts and providing support and guidance to help them achieve their goals. It can involve providing specific feedback on what the individual has done well and offering suggestions for improvement. Encouragement helps individuals to think critically about their actions, and to develop a sense of self-awareness and self-motivation.

On the other hand, praise can often be more general and may not provide specific feedback on what the individual has done well. It can also be more focused on the approval of others, rather than on the individual's own efforts and progress. When praise becomes the primary form of reinforcement, individuals may become overly reliant on external approval and may struggle to evaluate their own actions and progress. This can hinder their personal growth and development, as they may become less motivated to take risks and try new things.

Therefore, using encouragement can be more beneficial for personal growth and development, as it helps individuals to think more critically about their actions and to develop a stronger sense of self-awareness and self-motivation.

HOW WE CHOOSE WORDS

The choice of words can make a big difference in the type of feedback that is being given. Here are some additional examples of statements of encouragement versus statements of praise:

- "You worked really hard on that project, and it really paid off" versus "Great job on the project!"
- "I appreciate the way you were able to stay focused and complete the task" versus "You're so smart!"
- "I can see that you put a lot of effort into practicing your musical instrument, and it's really starting to show in your playing" versus "You're a natural at playing music!"

Statements of encouragement tend to focus on the individual's actions and efforts, and may also provide specific feedback on what the individual has done well. In contrast, statements of praise may be more general and may not provide as much information about the individual's actions and progress.

In Western culture, we tend to focus on praising others. Praise can be seen as similar to a sweet treat, in that a small amount can be very effective, but too much can have negative effects. It is common for adults to naturally praise young children. It is crucial to understand the distinction between encouragement and praise and how they can impact children.

Praise can be a powerful tool for reinforcing positive behavior and building self-esteem in children. However, it is important to use praise in a way that is authentic and specific, rather than vague or excessive.

Encouragement, on the other hand, is a more general form of positive reinforcement that focuses on supporting and motivating a child, rather than specifically praising a particular behavior or achievement. Encouragement can take many forms, such as providing a supportive and positive learning environment, offering words of support and reassurance, and helping children develop coping strategies for handling challenges and setbacks.

One key distinction between praise and encouragement is that praise tends to focus on the child's innate qualities or abilities, while encouragement focuses on the child's efforts and progress. For example, praising a child for being "smart" or "talented" may give them a boost of confidence in the short term, but it may also lead them to believe that their worth is tied to their innate abilities rather than their hard work and effort. On the other hand, encouraging a child to keep trying and persevere in the face of challenges helps them develop a growth mindset, which is the belief that their abilities can be developed through hard work and effort.

FINDING THE BALANCE

It is important to find the right balance between praise and encouragement in order to support and motivate children in a healthy way. Too much praise can lead to overconfidence and a sense of entitlement, while too little praise can lead to low self-esteem and a lack of motivation. It is important to recognize and praise children for their efforts and progress, rather than just their innate qualities or achievements.

Research has shown that the way in which we praise and encourage children can have a significant impact on their motivation and performance. Specifically, those who are praised for their innate qualities, such as being "smart," may be more likely to choose easier tasks and avoid challenges or mistakes in order to maintain their self-image as "smart" individuals. On the other hand, those who are encouraged for their efforts, progress, and improvement are more likely to take on challenging tasks and view mistakes as opportunities to learn and grow.

The language we use when praising or encouraging children can have a subtle but meaningful impact on their motivation and mindset. Focusing on a child's efforts, rather than their innate qualities, helps them see themselves as in control of their success and reinforces a growth mindset. Encouragement that focuses on factors such as effort, contribution, improvement, enjoyment, and confidence can help children feel more motivated and resilient.

It can be more effective to shift from saying "I like" to saying "I notice" when praising or encouraging children. This change in language helps children focus on their own efforts and progress, rather than seeking approval or validation from others. Asking a question or using language that prompts self-reflection, such as "I notice that you worked hard on that project. What strategies did you use to solve the problem?" can help children think more deeply about their own efforts and progress. This can ultimately be more motivating and empowering than simply stating a fact or expressing approval.

Using language that prompts self-reflection and encourages children to think more deeply about their own efforts and progress can be a powerful tool for motivation and learning. When we say, "I like," we are expressing approval or validation, which can be gratifying for children, but it does not necessarily encourage them to think about their own actions or progress. On the other hand, when we say, "I notice," we are drawing attention to something specific and encouraging children to think about what they did or what happened.

For example, instead of saying "I like the way you colored in the picture," you might say, "I notice that you used a lot of different colors in your picture. Can you tell me about your choices and how you decided which colors to use?" This shift in language prompts the child to think more deeply about their own actions and decision-making process, rather than simply seeking approval or validation.

Asking questions that prompt self-reflection and encourage children to think more deeply about their efforts and progress can be a powerful tool for motivation and learning. It helps children develop a sense of ownership and control over their own success, which can be more empowering and motivating than simply receiving approval or validation.

Shifting from saying "I like" to saying "I notice" when praising or encouraging children can change the parent-child dynamic by shifting the focus from the parent's approval to the child's own efforts and progress. When we say, "I like," we are expressing approval or validation, which can be gratifying for children, but it also puts the focus on the parent's perspective and judgment. On the other hand, when we say, "I notice," we are drawing attention to something specific and encouraging children to think about what they did or what happened. This shift in language helps children focus on their own efforts and progress, rather than seeking approval or validation from their parents.

This change in dynamic can be especially important when it comes to building children's self-esteem and motivation. When children feel that their worth is tied to the approval of others, they may become overly reliant on external validation and less motivated to take on challenges or try new things. On the other hand, when children are encouraged to focus on their own efforts and progress, they are more likely to develop a sense of ownership and control over their own success, which can be more empowering and motivating.

This change in dynamic can also help strengthen the connection between parent and child by creating a more supportive and positive environment for learning and growth. When children feel that their worth is tied to the approval of others, they may be less motivated to take on challenges or try new things. On the other hand, when children are encouraged to focus on their own efforts and progress, they are more likely to feel motivated and empowered to take on challenges and pursue their goals.

Overall, shifting from "I like" to "I notice" can help create a more positive and supportive parent-child dynamic that focuses on children's efforts, progress, and growth.

ACKNOWLEDGING A CHILD'S EFFORTS

It is important to acknowledge and recognize children's efforts in order to support and motivate them in their learning and development. Acknowledging effort involves not only noticing and pointing out when children are working hard but also showing appreciation and respect for the effort they are putting in. This can be a powerful tool for building self-esteem, motivation, and a growth mindset.

There are many different ways that parents and care-givers can acknowledge children's efforts: Notice and point out effort: Pay attention to the effort that children are putting into their work and let them know that you notice. This can be as simple as saying "I see that you're working hard on that puzzle" or "You've been practicing your reading a lot lately. I'm proud of you.".

Show appreciation and respect: Let children know that you appreciate and respect the effort they are putting in. This can involve verbal praise, such as saying, "Your hard work is paying off" or "I'm so proud of your determination," as well as nonverbal cues, such as a smile or a hug.

Provide opportunities for challenge and growth: Encourage children to take on challenges and stretch themselves by providing opportunities for growth and learning. This can involve introducing new material or activities, or encouraging children to take on age-appropriate responsibilities. Help children develop coping strategies: Encourage children to persevere in the face of challenges or setbacks by helping them develop coping strategies, such as problem-solving or seeking help when needed.

Encourage self-reflection: Encourage children to reflect on their own efforts and progress by asking questions or providing prompts for self-reflection. For example, you might say, "What strategies did you use to solve that problem?" or "How did you feel when you finished that project?"

By acknowledging and recognizing children's efforts, parents and caregivers can help build self-esteem, motivation, and a growth mindset, which can ultimately help children achieve their full potential.

Connecting children's efforts to their development is an important aspect of supporting and motivating children in their learning and growth. When children understand how their efforts contribute to their development, they are more likely to be motivated and engaged in their learning.

There are several ways that parents and caregivers can connect children's efforts to their development:

- **Make the connection explicit**: Help children understand the link between their efforts and their development by making the connection explicit. For example, you might say, "Your hard work on math is helping you build important problem-solving skills" or "Practicing your reading is helping you build your vocabulary and improve your comprehension."

- **Provide feedback and encouragement**:
Provide regular feedback and encouragement
to help children understand how their efforts
are paying off and contributing to their
development. This can involve praising specific
efforts or behaviors, such as "I'm so proud of
the effort you put into studying for that test" or
"Your persistence in learning to ride a bike is
really paying off."

- **Set goals and track progress**: Setting goals and
tracking progress can help children see the
progress they are making and understand how
their efforts are contributing to their
development. This can involve setting specific,
measurable, achievable, relevant, and time-
bound (SMART) goals and tracking progress
toward those goals.

- **Encourage self-reflection**: Encourage children
to reflect on their own efforts and progress by
asking questions or providing prompts for self-
reflection. This can help children develop a
sense of ownership and control over their own
development and encourage a growth mindset.

- **Provide a supportive learning environment**:
Create a supportive learning environment that
encourages effort and progress. This can
involve providing a range of learning materials

and activities, offering encouragement and support, and helping children develop coping strategies for handling challenges and setbacks.

By connecting children's efforts to their development and providing a supportive and encouraging learning environment, parents and caregivers can help children feel motivated and engaged in their learning and growth.

In order to recognize and acknowledge children's efforts, it is important to pay close attention to the details of their actions and the time and effort they are putting in. Consider the following:

What are children doing? Look closely at the details and actions involved in their efforts.

How much time are children spending on their actions? This can give you an idea of the level of effort and dedication they are putting in.

Is this a repeat choice of action for the child? If a child is consistently choosing to engage in a particular activity, it may be an indication of their interest and motivation.

What skills, resources, and steps are children using? Observing the strategies and tools children are using can give you insight into their progress and development.

What areas of development are being explored? Look for opportunities for children to develop new skills and knowledge in a variety of areas, such as social, emotional, physical, and cognitive development.

What do children seem to know or want to know? Pay attention to children's questions and curiosity, as this can give you insight into their interests and motivations.

By paying close attention to children's efforts and considering these factors, you can better recognize and acknowledge the importance and meaning of their efforts for the child.

There are several ways that you can use language to acknowledge and recognize children's efforts:

- **Use positive body language**: When acknowledging children's efforts, be physically present and make eye contact to show that you are paying attention and are interested.
- **Listen actively**: Listen carefully to what children are saying and reflect on their words to show that you are taking their efforts seriously.

- **Use open-ended questions**: Ask open-ended questions that prompt children to think and reflect on their efforts, rather than simply providing one-word answers. This can help you gather more information about their efforts and engage them in the conversation.
- **Reflect the effort and actions**: Use language to reflect and describe the specific actions and efforts that children are putting in. For example, you might say, "I see that you put a lot of effort into planning and organizing your project. Can you tell me more about your process?"
- **Document the effort**: Keep notes, photographs, videos, or other records of children's efforts to help recognize and acknowledge their progress.
- **Provide time and resources**: Make sure to provide children with the time, materials, and experiences they need to support their efforts. This can involve setting aside dedicated time for learning and providing access to a range of learning materials and activities.

By using language that is supportive, attentive, and reflective, you can help acknowledge and recognize children's efforts in a way that is meaningful and motivating.

One of the most effective ways to acknowledge and recognize children's efforts is to provide ample time and support for their work and play. This can involve being flexible with your schedule and setting aside dedicated time for children to explore their interests and engage in learning activities. By providing plenty of time for children's efforts, you can help create a supportive environment that encourages discovery and meaningful experiences.

Polishing your skills of recognizing and acknowledging children's efforts is an important aspect of supporting their learning and development. By paying attention to the details of children's actions, listening actively, and using language that reflects and supports their efforts, you can help guide their discovery and contribute to meaningful experiences that are motivating and empowering.

To conclude, acknowledging and recognizing children's efforts is an important aspect of supporting and motivating them in their learning and development. By paying attention to the details of children's actions, using supportive and reflective language, and providing plenty of time and resources to support their work and play, parents and caregivers can help create a supportive and empowering environment that encourages growth and development. By polishing their skills of recognizing and acknowledging children's efforts, parents and caregivers can help guide children's discoveries and contribute to meaningful experiences that are motivating and empowering.

Recognizing and acknowledging children's efforts is an important part of supporting their learning and development. When children feel that their efforts are valued and appreciated, they are more likely to be motivated and engaged in their learning.

In this chapter, parents have learned about the difference between encouragement and praise, and the impact they have on children's self-esteem and motivation. This chapter discussed how encouragement can foster a growth mindset, self-motivation, and self-esteem in children, and provides examples of ways parents can encourage their children and tips for making it a part of daily interactions.

The next chapter in the book builds upon the theme of setting limits and discipline. This chapter will discuss the importance of understanding and acknowledging children's emotions while enforcing consequences. It will cover the concept of natural consequences, logical consequences, and how to communicate them with empathy and understanding. Parents will learn how to provide consequences that are effective in teaching responsibility and self-discipline while avoiding harsh or punitive measures. The chapter will also include examples of different types of consequences and when it is appropriate to use each one and also ways to explain consequences in a way that children can understand and learn from.

7

CONSEQUENCES WITH EMPATHY

As parents, it's important to set boundaries and limits for our children to help them understand right from wrong and the natural consequences of their actions. But discipline can be a tricky thing, especially when it comes to finding the right balance between being firm and understanding. One way to approach this is through the use of consequences with empathy, a parenting method that involves setting limits and boundaries for children, but also approaching the situation with empathy and understanding, trying to see things from the child's perspective, and helping them to develop problem-solving skills.

Consequences with empathy mean that while being consistent and firm in enforcing consequences, parents approach the situation by understanding the child's feelings, thoughts, and motivations that led to the behavior, hence providing an opportunity for the child to learn and grow.

This approach can help children learn and grow and can foster a positive, supportive relationship between parents and children. It can help children understand their actions and think about the potential consequences of their actions, which can help them make better choices in the future.

In this chapter, we will explore the importance of consequences with empathy and how they can be used effectively in different situations. We will also provide practical strategies for how to set limits and boundaries for children, while also approaching situations with empathy and understanding. Through this chapter, you will gain a better understanding of how to use consequences with empathy to help your child learn, grow, and develop problem-solving skills, all while fostering a positive and supportive relationship with them.

WHAT ARE THE CONSEQUENCES OF EMPATHY?

Consequences with empathy is a parenting approach that involves setting boundaries and limits for children, and helping them to understand and learn from the natural consequences of their actions. It is important for parents to be firm and consistent in enforcing consequences, but also to approach the situation with empathy and understanding, trying to see things from the child's perspective and helping them to develop problem-solving skills. This approach can be effective in helping children to learn and grow and can foster a positive, supportive relationship between parents and children.

This approach can be an effective way for children to learn and grow, as they are able to directly experience the results of their choices and behaviors. For example, if a child consistently fails to arrive on time, they may miss out on events or activities as a consequence. While it is important for parents to be firm in enforcing consequences, it is also important to approach the situation with empathy, showing understanding and support as the child navigates the challenge and learning process. By providing empathy and support, parents can help children to develop problem-solving skills and resilience, ultimately helping them to become more responsible and self-sufficient.

HOW TO SUPPORT OUR CHILDREN THROUGH CONSEQUENCES WITH EMPATHY?

There are many different ways in which we can support our children when parenting using consequences with empathy. These methods can all help our children to adjust to life with consequences more easily if this is something they were previously unfamiliar with.

Setting clear boundaries and limits can be an important part of parenting, as it helps children to understand what is expected of them and what behaviors are acceptable. This can help to prevent misunderstandings and conflicts and can provide a sense of structure and security for children. When setting boundaries and limits, it is important for parents to be consistent and clear, so that children know what to expect and can learn to make good choices. It is also important for parents to be reasonable and fair, and to be willing to listen to their children's thoughts and feelings. By establishing clear boundaries and limits, parents can help their children to feel safe, secure, and confident, and can encourage them to take appropriate risks and make responsible decisions.

Helping children to understand the consequences of their actions is an important part of parenting, as it can help children to learn from their experiences and to make better choices in the future. When children make choices or behave in ways that have negative consequences, it is important for parents to help them understand the connection between their actions and the results. This can involve explaining the cause-and-effect relationship in a clear and age-appropriate way and helping children to see things from different perspectives. For example, if a child fails to complete their homework, the consequence might be a lower grade or a reprimand from the teacher. By helping children to understand the link between their actions and the consequences, parents can encourage children to think more carefully about their choices and to consider the potential outcomes of their actions. This can help children to develop problem-solving skills and to become more responsible and self-sufficient.

Showing empathy when children are experiencing the consequences of their actions is an important part of parenting, as it can help children feel understood and supported during difficult times. When children are facing a challenge or dealing with a difficult situation, it is important for parents to approach the situation with empathy and understanding. This can involve acknowledging the child's feelings and expressing genuine concern for their well-being. Parents can also provide comfort and support by listening actively and offering guidance and encouragement. By showing empathy, parents can help children to feel less alone and more supported, which can in turn help them to cope with the challenge they are facing and to learn and grow from the experience.

Encouraging problem-solving skills is an important part of the consequences of an empathetic approach to parenting, as it can help children to develop independence, resilience, and self-sufficiency. When children are facing a challenge or dealing with a difficult situation, it is important for parents to encourage them to think about how they might prevent similar situations from occurring in the future and to come up with solutions to the problems they are facing. This can involve asking open-ended questions, such as "What could you do differently next time?", and encouraging children to brainstorm and consider different options. By helping children to develop problem-solving skills, parents can encourage children to take an active role in finding solutions to their problems, rather than relying on others to solve their problems for them. This can help children to become more confident, responsible, and capable, and can foster a sense of pride and accomplishment.

Fostering a positive, supportive relationship with children is an important part of parenting, and can be especially important when it comes to using consequences with empathy. By approaching consequences with empathy, parents can help to create a supportive and understanding environment, in which children feel safe, valued, and heard. This can involve showing interest and concern for their well-being and being available to listen and offer guidance when needed. It can also involve demonstrating respect and appreciation for their thoughts and feelings, and being willing to compromise and negotiate when appropriate. By fostering a positive, supportive relationship with their children, parents can help children to feel more secure, confident, and resilient, and can encourage them to develop positive relationships with others.

IMPOSING CONSEQUENCES

As an alternative to allowing children to experience the natural consequences of their actions, parents can sometimes choose to impose consequences themselves. This can involve taking specific actions to coordinate or arrange things in a way that ensures the appropriate consequences follow certain actions. However, it is important for parents to be careful when imposing consequences, as they may be too lenient or too harsh if they are not careful. For example, if a child fails to complete their homework, a parent might decide to impose a consequence such as taking away screen time or requiring extra help with the subject. It is important for parents to consider the child's age, maturity level, and individual circumstances when deciding on an appropriate consequence, and to communicate clearly with the child about the reason for the consequence and what is expected of them.

When parents decide to impose consequences themselves, it is important to ensure that they are relevant to the misbehavior and that they are enforced in a consistent and non-threatening way. These imposed consequences should not be seen as traditional punishment, but rather as a tool to teach children about the connection between their actions and the results. The key is to make sure that the consequences are appropriate for the misbehavior, and that the child can understand how it relates to their actions. For example, if a child throws a toy, a relevant consequence could be having the toy taken away for a period of time, and then discussing with the child about how throwing the toy is not an appropriate way to express emotions. This way, the child will understand that actions have consequences and how the behavior is problematic.

It's also crucial that parents impose the consequences with a positive attitude, showing love, support, and understanding of the child, rather than anger or a threat. By doing so, parents can help children to understand the importance of taking responsibility for their actions and to learn to make better choices in the future. By making the consequences relevant and non-threatening, parents can make them more effective in teaching children valuable life lessons.

Let's look at a real-life example of consequences with empathy: Meet Sarah and her daughter, Samantha. Samantha has always been a picky eater and is particularly resistant to trying new foods. This has been a source of frustration for Sarah, who wants her daughter to have a well-balanced diet. One day, Sarah decides to set a rule that Samantha must at least try one new food at each meal.

However, when it comes time to enforce the rule, Sarah realizes that simply punishing Samantha for not trying a new food would not be effective. Instead, she decides to approach the situation with empathy. She talks to Samantha about her fears and concerns about trying new foods and listens to her daughter's perspective.

Samantha expresses that she's scared of the new taste and texture, so Sarah proposes a plan: They'll try new foods together and make it a fun game. They set a goal for trying one new food every week and make a chart to track their progress. They also look for recipes or new food presentations that will make it more interesting for her daughter.

As a consequence, if Samantha refused to try the new food or made a fuss, they'll skip the dessert. But if Samantha tried the food and didn't like it, they'll still have dessert, but she needs to put a smiley face on the chart, to represent the effort she put into trying it.

By using consequences in combination with empathy and understanding, Sarah is able to address the root of the problem and help her daughter develop healthy eating habits, and also helped her daughter to be more open-minded about new foods. This approach also helps to build a stronger relationship between mother and daughter as Samantha will know that her feelings are understood and respected.

In this example, the parent uses positive reinforcement and empathy to address a difficult issue and also create a way to communicate and track the progress, this can be helpful for other parents who might have similar challenges with their child with picky eating.

In the example I provided, Sarah, a parent, is struggling with her daughter Samantha's picky eating habits. As a parent, Sarah wants to ensure that her daughter has a well-balanced diet and she sets a rule that Samantha must at least try one new food at each meal. However, instead of simply punishing Samantha for not trying a new food, Sarah decides to approach the situation with empathy.

Sarah starts by having a conversation with Samantha about her fears and concerns about trying new foods. This allows Sarah to gain a better understanding of Samantha's perspective and where her reluctance to try new foods is coming from. Through this conversation, Sarah learns that Samantha is scared of the new taste and texture of foods, which is causing her to be resistant to trying them.

To help her daughter overcome this fear and develop healthy eating habits, Sarah proposes a plan to try new foods together, making it into a fun game. They set a goal for trying one new food every week and make a chart to track their progress. Also, they look for recipes or new food presentations that will make it more interesting for her daughter.

As a consequence, if Samantha refused to try the new food or made a fuss, they'll skip the dessert. But if Samantha tried the food and didn't like it, they'll still have dessert, but she needs to put a smiley face on the chart, to represent the effort she put into trying it. This consequence is fair and related to the rule that was broken, so Samantha understands why she needs to follow it, and it would be easier for her to comply with it.

It's also important to celebrate and recognize Samantha's progress and improvement. Sarah could give her special praise or a reward when she tried new food to maintain her motivation and positive reinforcement.

Overall, this example demonstrates how a parent can use consequences in combination with empathy and understanding to address a difficult issue and help a child develop important skills or habits. By taking an empathetic approach, Sarah is able to understand and address the root of the problem, and by setting clear consequences, she is able to provide the structure and support her daughter needs to be successful. And also it's important to track the progress and celebrate the improvement to maintain motivation.

THE IMPACT OF CRITICISM

It is not uncommon for children to experience blame, punishment, and criticism as part of their upbringing, but it can have a significant negative impact on their emotional well-being. Being constantly criticized or blamed can cause children to feel emotionally distressed and overwhelmed, making it difficult for them to access their cognitive and thinking abilities. The constant negative emotions can also prevent them from being able to think clearly and rationally, making it challenging for them to empathize with others or take their feelings into consideration.

When children are in emotional distress, it can affect the way their brain functions and changes the way they process information. Studies have shown that high levels of stress and negative emotions can lead to reduced activity in the prefrontal cortex, which is the part of the brain responsible for attention, impulse control, and reasoning. This means that children who are experiencing emotional distress may have difficulty paying attention and making good decisions, and may struggle with impulse control.

It is important for parents and caregivers to recognize the impact that negative feedback and punishment can have on children's emotional well-being and to use a more positive and empathetic approach in their parenting. This can include providing children with praise and positive reinforcement when they do well, giving clear and consistent explanations for rules and consequences, and taking the time to understand and address the underlying causes of behavior problems. By using a more empathetic and understanding approach, parents can help children develop important life skills and build positive relationships with others, while also promoting good mental health and well-being.

It is crucial that parents and caregivers remain connected and supportive during challenging and emotional situations with children. When a child is going through a difficult experience, it can be over-whelming for them to process and understand their feelings. By providing emotional support and guidance through these situations, parents can help children navigate these complex emotions and ultimately make their way back to feeling connected with their parents.

During these moments, it is essential for parents to remain supportive and understanding, rather than becoming critical or dismissive of the child's feelings. This can help children feel safe and secure enough to express their emotions and begin to work through them.

When a child has the space and support to process their feelings, they will be in a better position to take responsibility in a meaningful way. They will be more able to think clearly and make decisions based on sincerity, moral integrity, and clear thinking. It's an essential step for the child to take before making responsible decisions, acting on them, and accepting the consequences.

In summary, providing emotional support and connection during difficult situations is crucial for helping children process their emotions and ultimately take on more responsibilities with a clear understanding and good intentions. This not only helps children develop important life skills but also helps them to build positive relationships with their parents, promote mental well-being, and encourage moral integrity.

Being able to effectively handle and respond to your child's mistakes, failures, and setbacks is a crucial ability for parents to develop. Whether it's a loss in a soccer match, defeat by a sibling or friend in a board game, a poor report card, or any other kind of disappointment, your child will inevitably face challenges throughout their life. Your reactions and responses in these situations can greatly impact their social and emotional growth and development.

As a parent, it's important to recognize the impact that your reactions to your child's failures can have on their ability to cope with setbacks and move forward. Your reactions can play a significant role in shaping your child's resilience and self-confidence, as well as their ability to handle mistakes and failures throughout their lifetime. It's important to be aware of how your reactions can influence your child's future mindset and behavior.

It's important for parents to find effective ways to communicate to their children that experiencing failure does not reflect their intelligence or capability. One can use various approaches to convey this message to their child, to ensure that they understand and internalize it. Some examples might include emphasizing the learning opportunities that come from failure, praising their effort and perseverance, and helping them develop a growth mindset.

EMBRACING MISTAKES AND FAILURE

It can be difficult for parents to see their children fail or make mistakes, but allowing them to navigate and learn from these experiences is a crucial aspect of good parenting. Failure and mistakes offer valuable learning opportunities, which can help children develop resilience and build self-confidence. Without the chance to experience failure, children may have low self-esteem, lack problem-solving skills, and be hesitant to take risks or try new things. When kids are allowed the space to learn and grow through their mistakes, it can help to enhance their social and emotional development as well.

As a parent, it can be difficult to watch your child struggle and make mistakes, but it is an essential part of their growth and development. This does not mean neglecting to assist with homework, failing to provide reassurance, or ignoring when your child is in danger. However, it does mean allowing them to make some mistakes and learning from the consequences.

When your child faces a challenging situation, consider if it is necessary for you to intervene or if this is an opportunity for them to problem-solve and learn. Giving your child some autonomy and space to make age-appropriate decisions, even if it means they may fail, helps foster their independence and teaches them important lessons about failure and its role in life.

If children are accustomed to open and honest communication and have been taught to solve problems with their parents, they are more likely to offer possible solutions, provide reassurance, and express regret for their actions. However, if children are accustomed to being reprimanded or lectured for their mistakes, they may be more likely to be defensive when faced with problems.

When there is tension or negative emotions present in the parent-child relationship in situations related to mistakes or failures, it can lead to children feeling distressed and defensive, which affects their ability to truly listen, empathize and take accountability for their actions. This emotional state can inhibit their ability to think critically and come up with solutions, ultimately hindering their ability to learn from the experience and grow. Without these learning opportunities, they may miss out on key developments in their emotional and problem-solving skills. It is crucial for parents to recognize and address the emotional dynamics present in order to create a supportive environment for learning and growth.

In conclusion, it's important for parents to recognize and address the emotional dynamics present in situations related to mistakes and failures in order to create a supportive environment for learning and growth. When parents respond with empathy and understanding, they can help their children process their emotions and take responsibility for their actions. This allows children to learn from their mistakes and failures, develop resilience, and build self-confidence. By prioritizing empathy in their parenting, parents can set their children up for success in navigating the challenges of life, and developing their problem-solving, emotional, and social skills.

In this chapter, parents learned about the importance of understanding and acknowledging children's emotions while enforcing consequences. This chapter covered the concept of natural consequences, logical consequences, and how to communicate them with empathy and understanding. Parents have learned how to provide consequences that are effective in teaching responsibility and self-discipline while avoiding harsh or punitive measures. Examples of different types of consequences and when it is appropriate to use each one were also provided, as ways to explain consequences in a way that children can understand and learn from.

The next chapter in this book is a natural progression from the previous chapter, as it talks about the importance of parents being good role models for their children. The chapter explores how a parent's actions and behavior influence their children and how parents can be mindful of their own behavior to ensure they are setting a positive example. It will also discuss the importance of integrity and consistency in parenting, and how a parent's words and actions should align. The chapter also provides examples and strategies for parents to reflect on their own behavior and work towards being the best role model for their children.

8

ROLE MODELING

As parents, we are not only responsible for providing guidance and support to our children, but we also serve as role models for their behavior and attitudes. Our children look up to us, and they learn how to navigate the world by observing our actions and attitudes. The way we interact with others, handle stress, and approach challenges set the tone for our children's own behaviors and attitudes.

Role modeling is not just about setting a good example for our children, but it's also about self-awareness and being mindful of the message we are sending to our children through our own actions. As role models, parents must be aware of their own biases, emotions, and behaviors, as well as take active steps to change them if they are not in line with what they want to teach their children.

Effective role modeling means being intentional about the behaviors and attitudes we want to pass on to our children and making a conscious effort to embody those qualities. It means being mindful of the messages we are sending to our children through our words and actions, and making sure they align with the values and morals we want to instill in them.

It is also important to remember that role modeling doesn't mean that parents must be perfect and infallible, but it is about being honest, authentic, and apologizing when we make mistakes. Showing vulnerability and humility allows children to see that parents are also capable of making mistakes but can take responsibility for them and learn from them.

Role modeling is one of the most powerful and effective ways of teaching children responsibility and positive behavior. As parents, our own habits and behavior serve as a constant guide for our children, and they learn through watching us, not by what we say. By being a good role model and consistently demonstrating responsible behavior and good habits, we can help our children develop a strong sense of responsibility and a positive outlook on life.

The importance of role modeling in parenting cannot be overstated. Children are great imitators, and they pay attention to everything we do and say, from our actions and interactions with others to the words we use and the tone of our voice. We must be aware that they are constantly watching and listening, and that our behavior directly influences their values and beliefs.

HOW TO BE AN EFFECTIVE ROLE MODEL

One of the most effective ways to be a good role model is to consistently demonstrate responsible behavior and good habits. This might include being punctual and reliable, following through on commitments, being respectful and kind to others, and treating others with dignity and respect, regardless of their background or circumstances. We should also try to model appropriate behavior in our interactions with others and be mindful of the language we use and the opinions we express.

It is also important to create a safe and supportive environment for our children, one that is characterized by selfless love, firm but flexible limits, and open communication. By providing a safe and nurturing environment, we can help our children develop a sense of security and self-worth, and create the conditions that will allow them to thrive.

Another key aspect of being a good role model is to listen to your children when they are upset, try not to judge, and share your experiences and feelings with them. Try to make connections with your children, tell them about some of your past decision-making examples, and allow them to ask questions, you can use this as a guide for them in the future.

In addition to role-modeling and creating a safe and supportive environment, connecting with our children is also crucial for positive parenting. Building strong, positive relationships with our children is essential for helping them develop healthy self-esteem, build trust, and feel safe and secure. One way to connect with our children is to spend quality time with them, doing activities that they enjoy and that we can both participate in. This can help create shared memories and build a sense of closeness and connection.

It's also important to be responsive to our children's emotional needs and to be there for them when they need our help. This means listening to them, offering support and understanding, and being patient and empathetic. It's important to remember that children have their own unique personalities and need to be treated with respect and understanding.

In summary, as parents, we play a vital role in shaping the behavior and attitudes of our children. By serving as positive role models, creating a safe and supportive environment, and connecting with our children emotionally, we can help them develop into responsible and well-adjusted individuals. While we may not be perfect, by being self-aware, intentional, and humble, we can pass on valuable lessons and qualities to our children that will serve them well throughout their lives.

MODELING FOR OUR CHILDREN IN PRACTICAL LIFE

Modeling behavior is an important concept that helps children understand how to interact with others and navigate the world around them. It is the process of observing and imitating the actions of others in order to learn and develop new skills and behaviors. It is a natural way for children to learn and is something that happens every day, both at home and in school.

In practical life, children can model the behavior of their parents, siblings, teachers, and friends. They can learn how to tie their shoes by watching someone else do it, or learn how to be kind and considerate by observing the actions of a caring adult. Children can also learn valuable skills through observing and imitating the behavior of others in real-life situations, such as how to take turns, wait in line, or share toys.

Modeling behavior is also important for children to understand the consequences of their actions. If a child sees someone else being punished for misbehaving, they may be less likely to repeat that behavior themselves.

By helping children understand the concept of modeling behavior and encouraging them to observe and imitate the actions of positive role models, parents and teachers can help them develop the skills and behaviors they need to succeed in life.

It's important to point out that children model not just what people do, but also what they say and even how they react to certain situations. And that not only good behavior should be modeled, but also the learning process itself, how to solve problems, how to have empathy, how to communicate effectively, etc.

Modeling behavior to a child in practical life can be done in several ways. Here are a few examples:

1. Show, don't tell: Children learn by observing and imitating the actions and behaviors of adults around them. So, it's important to consistently model the behaviors and attitudes we want to teach them. For example, if you want to teach your child to be respectful and kind to others, you should make sure you are

consistently demonstrating those behaviors in your own interactions with others.

2. Use positive language: The words we use and the tone of our voice also serve as a model for our children. When talking to others, make sure to use positive, respectful language and avoid using negative or aggressive language.

3. Practice what you preach: Children can be very perceptive and will quickly pick up on any inconsistencies between what we say and what we do. It's important to practice what we preach and to make sure our actions align with our words.

4. Encourage independence: Children are naturally curious and want to learn new things. Encourage your child to try new things and make their own decisions as much as possible. This will help them develop self-confidence and self-reliance.

5. Emphasize positive attitudes: Share with them positive attitudes such as gratitude, perseverance, patience, and kindness.

6. Use scenarios to teach: Give real-life scenarios where the child can apply the learned behavior, like helping an elderly person cross the street, standing up for someone being bullied, helping out in chores and many more.

7. Show by example: when children see their parents demonstrating kindness, fairness, honesty, and other positive traits, they are more likely to adopt those same behaviors themselves.

8. Practice active listening and giving verbal feedback: Listen to your child when they express themselves, and use it as an opportunity to give them constructive feedback, and teach them to express their feelings and thoughts.

By consistently modeling the behaviors and attitudes we want to teach our children, using positive language, practicing what we preach, encouraging independence, and using real-life scenarios to teach, we can help our children develop positive behaviors and attitudes.

Modeling behavior for children is about more than just having them copy what we do or say. It's important to actively engage with children and help them understand the reasoning behind our actions and the way we express ourselves and our feelings. This can involve working closely with children and providing guidance and assistance as they learn to express themselves in new ways.

One important aspect of modeling behavior is helping children understand the choices and actions they make and how they can interact effectively with others. This can involve demonstrating how to communicate with others in a clear and empathetic way and explaining the importance of making good choices and considering the consequences of their actions.

It's essential to also mention that it is not only about not misbehaving but showing them how to problem-solve, how to be respectful, how to be a good listener and communicator, how to be empathetic, etc.

By showing and explaining why we do what we do, rather than simply telling children not to do something, we can empower them to make better choices and develop the skills they need to navigate the world around them. Teaching them the reasoning behind our actions is more powerful than just giving them commands.

THE IMPORTANCE OF EXPLANATIONS

Explaining things to children is important for a number of reasons. One of the most basic is that it helps them make sense of the world around them. Children are constantly learning and trying to understand the world, and when things are explained to them in a clear and simple way, it can help them to build a solid foundation of knowledge.

Additionally, explaining things to children can help to develop their critical thinking skills. When children are given an explanation, they can ask questions and explore the topic further, which helps them to think more critically about the information they are learning.

Explanations also help children to develop their language and communication skills. By talking with children and explaining things to them, you can help them to develop their vocabulary and improve their ability to express themselves. This is an important step in helping children to become good communicators, which is an important skill for both academic and social success.

Explaining also helps to improve their ability to follow directions and understand boundaries and consequences, it will help them to adapt to different social cues and environments, and also help them to build trust with adults.

Furthermore, when children understand why something is important or how something works, they are more likely to be interested and engaged in learning.

Finally, explaining things to children can help to build a strong parent-child relationship. When you take the time to explain things to your child, you are showing them that you value their understanding and that you are willing to take the time to help them learn. This can help to create a positive and supportive learning environment that encourages children to be curious and eager to learn more.

In summary, explaining things to children is important for helping them to make sense of the world, developing their critical thinking skills, improving their language and communication skills, building trust and following directions, fostering a positive attitude towards learning, and creating a positive and supportive environment for learning.

This chapter has helped us learn about the power of parents as role models. Our actions and behavior shape the way our children see the world and how they learn to navigate it. Children learn by watching and imitating their parents, so it's important that we lead by example in the way we treat others, handle difficult situations, and make responsible decisions.

We can help our children develop a sense of responsibility by giving them age-appropriate tasks and responsibilities, and providing guidance and support as needed. We can also teach them how to make responsible choices by setting clear rules and consequences, and by consistently enforcing them.

One important aspect of teaching responsibility is helping children understand the impact of their actions on others. We can encourage children to think about the consequences of their choices and to take ownership of their mistakes. By helping children learn how to take responsibility for their actions, we are laying the foundation for them to become responsible adults. We will discuss this more in the next chapter along with learning to choose and take responsibility is a lifelong process, children will make mistakes, but it's important to keep encouraging them to learn from those mistakes, and to continue to guide them on the path to becoming responsible adults.

9

LEARNING TO CHOOSE CREATES RESPONSIBILITY

I n this chapter, we will explore the importance of helping children learn to make responsible choices, and how this can help them develop a sense of responsibility. As parents, we play a vital role in teaching our children how to navigate the world and make sound decisions. By giving our children the tools they need to make responsible choices, we are helping to prepare them for a successful and fulfilling life.

We will discuss strategies for teaching children about the consequences of their actions, and how to take responsibility for their decisions. We will also explore ways to foster independence and autonomy in children, while still providing guidance and support.

By the end of this chapter, readers will have a better understanding of how to support their children in developing a sense of responsibility and will have practical strategies for doing so. It will also discuss the importance of being a role model for your children in making responsible choices and how it will positively impact your child in their journey to become a responsible adult.

Learning to make choices is an essential aspect of child development, as it helps children develop a sense of responsibility and learn about the consequences of their actions. Giving children the opportunity to make choices allows them to gain control over their own lives and make decisions that are appropriate for their age and maturity level. When children are given choices, they feel a sense of agency and ownership over their actions.

Making choices also changes the dynamic between parent and child. Instead of being a battleground for control, choices allow parents to communicate with their children in a more constructive way. Instead of using words or actions that provoke resistance or power struggles, parents can use language that encourages children to think and make decisions for themselves. This helps children develop critical thinking and problem-solving skills that will serve them well as they grow older.

As children learn to make choices, they also learn to take responsibility for the outcomes of their decisions. They begin to understand that their actions have consequences and that they are responsible for the outcomes of their choices. This is a critical aspect of child development as it helps them learn to take ownership of their lives and become more independent.

Helping children learn to make choices is an important step in their development as it plays a vital role in building responsibility and self-sufficiency. By providing opportunities for children to make choices, parents can give them a sense of control over their own lives and help them develop decision-making skills that will serve them well as they grow older.

Allowing children to make choices also shifts the dynamic between parent and child, moving away from power struggles and conflicts toward a more collaborative and constructive relationship. Instead of focusing on enforcing rules and control, parents can use language and guidance that encourages children to think for themselves and make responsible decisions.

Through the process of making choices, children also learn about the consequences of their actions, which is an important part of developing personal responsibility. They start to understand that their actions have real-world outcomes and that they are responsible for the results of their decisions. This promotes a sense of self-awareness and ownership of their actions, which is a key aspect of becoming a responsible adult.

Overall, helping children learn to make choices is a powerful way to foster responsibility, self-sufficiency, and independent thinking. It promotes positive and constructive relationships between parents and children and helps children develop the skills they need to navigate the world and make responsible decisions as they grow up.

Adopting the approach of giving children choices in their decision-making can have a profound impact on their development. When children are given the opportunity to make choices, they learn to think critically, solve problems and develop decision-making skills. This helps them become more independent and self-sufficient.

Additionally, this approach promotes a positive dynamic between parents and children. By giving children choices, parents are demonstrating trust in their children's abilities, which builds self-confidence and strengthens the relationship between parent and child. Children feel valued and respected when given the opportunity to make choices, which can also build their self-esteem.

This approach also shifts the parent-child dynamic from a control-based one to one that is more cooperative and constructive. Children will learn to think and make decisions for themselves instead of being told what to do, and will not feel the need to resist their parents' demands, which helps create a more relaxed and peaceful environment.

In conclusion, the entire game changes when we apply this approach of giving children choices. They learn to think more and handle things better, and we, as parents, build a stronger and more trusting relationship with them by showing confidence in their abilities and treating them with respect and autonomy, which helps in their overall development as responsible individuals.

HOW TO TEACH RESPONSIBILITY THROUGH CHOICES

One way to teach children responsibility is by giving them choices and allowing them to experience the natural consequences of their actions.

For example, if your child has made a mess after a project, instead of demanding they clean it up, give them a choice. You can give them the option to clean up and continue with their project the next night, or neglect cleaning and be unable to continue the project or have access to their things the following night.

It is crucial for parents to follow through and hold their children accountable for their choices. If you enforce the rules and the natural consequences of their actions, children are more likely to learn the importance of cleaning up and taking responsibility for their actions.

Many parents may hesitate to let their children face negative consequences, but it is essential to understand that through experiencing the consequences, children learn responsibility and problem-solving skills. It's easy to tell them, but they learn best when they experience it themselves.

It is also important to balance nurturing with discipline, and children will learn to make responsible choices and take ownership of their actions. This approach can be challenging, but ultimately, it will help children grow into responsible adults.

It's vital to note that giving children choices and allowing them to experience the consequences of their actions is a key element in teaching responsibility, but it's not the only one. Along with providing choices, it's also essential for parents to provide guidance, support, and clear expectations. It's also important for parents to be consistent in enforcing rules and consequences. This helps children understand the importance of taking responsibility for their actions and the consequences that come with them.

Additionally, it's important for parents to model responsible behavior themselves. Children learn by example, and if parents model responsible behavior, children are more likely to adopt the same behavior. For example, parents should take responsibility for their own actions, apologize when they make a mistake, and admit when they are wrong.

It's also important for parents to acknowledge and praise their children when they make responsible choices. This positive reinforcement helps children understand the importance of taking responsibility for their actions and encourages them to continue making responsible choices.

In summary, teaching children responsibility involves a combination of giving them choices, providing guidance and support, enforcing rules and consequences consistently, modeling responsible behavior, and reinforcing responsible choices. It's a process that requires patience and commitment, but the end result is well worth it as children grow into responsible and self-sufficient adults.

When teaching children responsibility by giving them choices and allowing them to experience the consequences of their actions, it's important to be prepared for potential resistance and negativity. Children may not always like the consequences of their choices and may express dissatisfaction or frustration. However, it's important for parents to remain calm and consistent in enforcing rules and consequences.

TESTING THE BOUNDARIES

It's natural for children to push back and test boundaries, but it's important for parents to stay firm in their expectations and not give in to demands or pleadings. Giving in sends the message that rules and consequences are not important, and undermines the effectiveness of teaching responsibility.

It's important for parents to communicate with their children and explain why rules and consequences are in place. This helps children understand the reasoning behind them and how it relates to developing responsibility.

It's also important for parents to give their children space to process and deal with their emotions. It's normal for children to be upset, but it's important to give them time to reflect on the consequences of their actions and understand how it relates to their behavior.

All in all, as parents, it's important to be prepared for potential opposition and unhappiness from children when teaching responsibility through choices and consequences, but it's crucial to maintain a calm and consistent approach, stay firm in your expectations and rules, communicate the reasoning behind them and give children space to process their emotions. This will ultimately help them learn the importance of taking responsibility for their actions.

Implementing a system of giving children choices and allowing them to experience the consequences of their actions can be a challenging task for parents. It's important to remember that the process may require patience and consistency, and it's not always easy to stay calm when children are upset or when things don't go as planned.

It's important for parents to avoid getting angry or adding more negative emotions to the situation. This can nullify the benefits of the process and make it more difficult for children to learn from their choices and consequences. Instead, parents should maintain a neutral and firm demeanor, and stick to the rules and consequences that were previously established.

It's also important to keep in mind that consequences don't always have to be immediate. Depending on the situation and the child's age, it may be necessary to allow more time for consequences to take effect. It's important to be patient and let the child learn from their choices in their own time.

In summary, teaching children responsibility through choices and consequences can be difficult for parents, but it's important to remember that the process requires patience, consistency, and maintaining a neutral and firm attitude. Avoiding anger or adding more negative emotions to the situation and being patient with the time the child needs to learn from their choices are key points to keep in mind for a successful outcome.

Another important aspect to consider when teaching children responsibility through choices and conse-quences is the use of empathy. While it is important for parents to enforce consequences and hold children accountable for their actions, it is also important to show compassion and support when children make mistakes.

Empathy involves putting ourselves in our children's shoes and understanding their perspectives. It is impor-tant to remember that children are still learning and developing and that they will inevitably make bad choices. When they do, it's important to help them understand the consequences of their actions and how they can learn from them.

Empathy also means showing understanding and support as children learn to accept responsibility for their actions. Children may be upset or discouraged by the consequences of their choices, but it's important to be there for them emotionally and provide guidance and support.

It's important to remember that even when children make bad choices, the goal is not to punish them, but rather to help them learn and grow from the experience. Empathy is a key component in this process, as it allows us to guide children through difficult experiences with understanding and compassion.

Overall, when teaching children responsibility through choices and consequences, it's important to use empathy as a key component in the overall plan. We still show compassion and moral support, but the choice is theirs and we can still help them to learn from their mistakes with humility and understanding, rather than punishing them.

In conclusion, helping children learn to make responsible choices is an essential part of their development. Giving children choices allows them to gain control over their own lives and make decisions that are appropriate for their age and maturity level. Through the process of making choices, children learn about the consequences of their actions, which helps them develop a sense of personal responsibility.

It is important to provide guidance, support, and clear expectations to children while providing them with choices and being consistent in enforcing rules and consequences. The process of teaching responsibility through choices also requires patience and understanding, as children learn and grow at their own pace. Empathy is a key component to understanding and supporting children as they learn to accept responsibility for their actions.

As parents, it is important to model responsible behavior ourselves. Children learn by example, and if parents model responsible behavior, children are more likely to adopt the same behavior.

Through this approach of giving choices and consequences, parents can help children develop the skills they need to navigate the world, make responsible decisions, and become independent, self-sufficient, and responsible adults.

CONCLUSION

In conclusion, positive parenting involves setting limits with connection in order to create a supportive and nurturing environment for children's learning and development. By setting clear expectations and boundaries, and communicating openly and honestly with children, parents and caregivers can create a structure that promotes healthy growth and development.

At the same time, it is important to maintain a strong connection with children and show them love, respect, and appreciation. This can involve praising children for their efforts and progress, rather than their innate qualities or achievements, and encouraging independence and self-reflection. By building a strong connection with children, parents and caregivers can create a supportive and nurturing environment that promotes healthy emotional development.

Effective positive parenting involves finding a balance between setting limits and maintaining a strong connection with children. This involves setting clear expectations and boundaries to provide structure and guidance, while also showing children love, respect, and appreciation.

Setting limits is an important aspect of positive parenting because it helps children understand what is expected of them and provides a sense of security and predictability. By setting clear expectations and consequences for behavior, parents and caregivers can help children develop self-control and self-regulation skills.

At the same time, it is important to maintain a strong connection with children and show them love, respect, and appreciation. This can involve praising children for their efforts and progress, rather than their innate qualities or achievements, and encouraging independence and self-reflection. By building a strong connection with children, parents and caregivers can create a supportive and nurturing environment that promotes healthy emotional development.

In addition to setting limits and maintaining a connection, effective positive parenting also involves open and honest communication. By being open and honest with children and listening actively to their needs and concerns, parents and caregivers can create a positive and supportive environment that promotes healthy communication and relationship-building.

Overall, positive parenting involves finding the right balance between setting limits and maintaining connections in order to create a supportive and nurturing environment that promotes healthy growth and development. By following these principles, parents and caregivers can help their children reach their full potential and lead happy, healthy, and fulfilling lives.

I hope that over the course of reading this book, you will have developed the tools needed to effectively parent your child using the special connection only a parent can develop. Now you have the tools needed to create a positive parenting experience for both you and your family to take on the world together. Don't be shy! Go out and seize the day with your family using the tools taught in this book!

If you have enjoyed reading this book and found the information useful then why not leave us a helpful Amazon review? By leaving a review you might be able to help another family on their parenting journey!

REFERENCES

Abramson, A. (2020, October 15). *The Science Behind Your Child's Tantrums*. The New York Times. https://www.nytimes.com/2020/10/15/parenting/kids-tantrums-advice.html

Arky, B. (n.d.). *How to Help Kids Learn to Fail*. Child Mind Institute. https://childmind.org/article/how-to-help-kids-learn-to-fail/

Canizares, S. (2022, June 6). *Responsibility and Making Good Choices*. Www.childtime.com. https://www.childtime.com/blog/2022/06/responsibility-and-making-good-choices/

Cataldo, S. (2021, February 12). *If We Want To Raise Resilient Children, We Need To Listen To Our Kids More*. Scary Mommy. https://www.scarymommy.com/resilient-child-stop-telling-kids-to-stop-crying

generic, Y. team. (2020, September 2). *How To Help Teens When They Make Bad Choices*. Spark Their Future. https://www.sparktheir future.qld.edu.au/why-teens-make-bad-choices-and-how-you-can-help-them/

Gfroerer, K. (n.d.). *What Is the Difference Between Praise and Encouragement?* Continued Early Childhood Education. Retrieved January 11, 2023, from https://www.continued.com/early-child hood-education/ask-the-experts/what-difference-between-praise-and-23704

Hamilton, M. (2019, January 21). *Why You Need to Stop Lecturing Your Kids (And What to Do Instead)*. A Fine Parent. https://afineparent. com/positive-parenting-faq/stop-lecturing-your-kids.html

Hartstein, Dr. J. (2017, September 15). *The Importance of Setting Limits for Your Child*. Hartstein Psychological Services. https://www.hart steinpsychological.com/importance-setting-limits-child

Krisbergh, A. (n.d.). *Being a Role Model - The Promise and the Peril*. The Center for Parenting Education. Retrieved January 11, 2023, from https://centerforparentingeducation.org/library-of-articles/focus-parents/role-model-promise-peril/

Lee, K. (2021, January 31). *How Should You React When Your Child Makes a Mistake?* Verywell Family. https://www.verywellfamily.com/what-to-do-when-your-child-makes-a-mistake-4050012

Markham, L. (n.d.). *What To Say Instead Of Punishing To Teach A Lesson.* Www.ahaparenting.com. Retrieved January 11, 2023, from https://www.ahaparenting.com/read/what-to-say-instead-of-punishing-to-teach-a-lesson

Nelson, Dr. J. (2021, May 2). *Connection Before Correction.* Www.positivediscipline.com. https://www.positivediscipline.com/articles/connection-correction-0

Penn State. (n.d.). *Acknowledging children's efforts (Better Kid Care).* Better Kid Care (Penn State Extension). Retrieved January 11, 2023, from https://extension.psu.edu/programs/betterkidcare/early-care/tip-pages/all/acknowledging-children2019s-efforts

Program, N. S. (2020, August 10). *Connecting in Times of Crisis: Eye Contact.* Nurture Science Program. https://nurturescienceprogram.org/connecting-despite-crisis-eye-contact/

Scheiner, A. C. (2010, June 4). *Effective Limit-Setting: Ideas for Parents.* Www.childandfamilymentalhealth.com. https://www.childandfamilymentalhealth.com/adhd/effective-limit-setting-ideas-for-parents/

Setting Clear Limits. (n.d.). Aidtolife.org. https://aidtolife.org/discipline/setting-limits.html

Simperingham, G. (2013, June 20). *Should we enforce consequences?* The Way of the Peaceful Parent. https://www.peacefulparent.com/should-we-enforce-consequences/

Special Playtime | Communicating with Your Child | Essentials | Parenting Information | CDC. (2020, June 8). Www.cdc.gov. https://www.cdc.gov/parents/essentials/communication/specialplaytime.html

Waheeda, A. (2020, November 10). *Why lecturing kids doesn't work (and what to do instead).* Messy, yet Lovely. https://messyyetlovely.com/stop-lecturing-kids/

CPSIA information can be obtained
at www.ICGtesting.com
Printed in the USA
LVHW051134130523
746921LV00016B/1560